CONTENTS

THE SIXTEEN PR(

Introduction 299

ISTJ: Life's Natural Organizers 302

ISFJ: Committed to Getting the Job Done 309

INFJ: An Inspiring Leader and Follower 314

INTJ: Life's Independent Thinkers 320

ISTP: Just Do It 325

ISFP: Action Speaks Louder Than Words 330

INFP: Making Life Kinder and Gentler 336

INTP: Life's Conceptualizers 341

ESTP: Making the Most of the Moment 347

ESFP: Let's Make Work Fun 352

ENFP: People Are the Product 358

ENTP: Progress Is the Product 363

ESTJ: Life's Natural Administrators 369

ESFJ: Everyone's Trusted Friend 374

ENFJ: Smooth-Talking Persuaders 379

ENTJ: Life's Natural Leaders 385

About Otto Kroeger Associates 390

INTRODUCTION

In our first book, *Type Talk*, we offered comprehensive profiles of the sixteen personality types, detailing their behavior throughout their lives—as children, parents, mates, even as senior citizens. The profiles that follow focus primarily on the relationships and situations of the workplace.

Be careful: The danger in creating typological profiles is that they are usually viewed as rigid boxes encompassing an unvarying and static set of characteristics. That can make them more confining than liberating, ironically defeating the whole point of Typewatching, which is to allow room for you to be yourself and for others to be themselves. We do not intend these profiles to be the final statements; rather they are intended as points of reference for insight into yourself and others. Remember the Third Commandment of Typewatching (see page 47): It is only a theory; it takes real life to validate it.

There are several ways to validate your profile. First and foremost is to highlight those parts with which you agree and note the parts with which you disagree. Next, you might consider soliciting feedback about your profile from those who know you well—your mate, your staff, your co-workers, perhaps even your kids. These individuals will confirm or counter what you saw about yourself in the profile; where they disagree with you will provide the basis for a highly insightful discussion about others' perceptions of you. Furthermore you might want to read the profile of your four-letter opposite—the ENFJ profile, for example, if you are an ISTP. Such a reading should provide a sharp contrast to your own preferences, helping to put your own profile into perspective.

Typological profiles have been accused from time to time of being like astrological horoscopes: general statements broad enough to encompass everyone. That's simply not true. These profiles are based on sound theory and empirical observation of human behavior.

Most of the Typewatching profiles previously written have been more positive than negative. This concurred with the affirming nature of Typewatching in general: It is a psychological model based on health and wellness rather than on sickness. The workplace-oriented profiles on the following pages break that trend. Because the workplace, with its stresses and demands, often engenders a variety of behaviors that are not all positive, and because people often get tripped up by the negative side of a boss or a subordinate, we felt it was important to spend some time describing the various weaknesses that can plague each type. We believe it is important to know the potential stumbling points if you are to be well equipped to deal with the demands of the workplace.

Still, there are many strengths to be found in each profile. The more we can integrate those strengths and recognize the shortfalls, the more we can live with—and even prosper from—each other's differences.

How to Use the Profiles

The profiles below can be useful in several ways:

- First and most important, they can validate your own personality type. Whether you have taken the Myers-Briggs Type Indicator or simply identified your four preferences from reading this book, the profiles can substantiate your findings, showing how the four letters interact to create a unique personality type. In reading your profile, if you find yourself agreeing with most of the statements, you have likely reported yourself accurately. It may be helpful as you read the profile to underline or highlight those parts with which you strongly agree or disagree.

- Next consider sharing your profile with someone who knows you well, perhaps a co-worker, boss, or subordinate. Consider asking that person to highlight the parts of your profile with which he or she strongly agrees or disagrees. That will give you some powerful feedback about whether others perceive you as you perceive yourself.

- This exercise can also work in a group situation. Sharing profiles, and having them available at crucial moments—before meetings, on deadline, during crises—can help keep lines of communication open and allow each individual to use his or her strengths and be mindful of particular weaknesses.

- Another possible use of the profiles is in coping with individuals who may be giving you difficulty at work. If you know—or can at least guess—their four preferences, reading their profiles may provide some insight into the source of the problem. That can open the way to communication and resolution.

ISTJ

Life's Natural Organizers

This is the quintessential dependable, responsible type—hence the quintessential manager. Just like the work world itself, ISTJs are driven by accountability, productivity, and the bottom line. It is a natural and often happy fit.

ISTJs see the world in terms of facts and tangible realities (Sensing), which they prefer to deal with in an objective fashion (Thinking). Their day-to-day living is driven by structure, schedule, and order (Judging), and their Introversion makes them appear somewhat cool and aloof. Appearances can be deceiving, however, because ISTJs often excel when it comes to achievement, accomplishment, and social skills.

ISTJ is a no-frills, work-hard, play-hard type. They are seen as compulsive, hard-charging, capable, and true to their word. They live by the bottom line and can be very cost-conscious. They can be slow to change, but once they see the practical value in making a course correction, they can be quick to implement it and often become zealots of the new way of thinking.

While all Thinking females swim upstream in our society, this is particularly true for female ISTJs. The responsible, driven nature of this type, while admirable, flies in the face of traditionally "feminine" traits. Moreover, as traditionalists at heart, ISTJ females are inwardly conflicted about trying to balance the conventional feminine roles— mothering and nurturing—with their objective, organized (TJ) nature. A typical response to this dilemma is to work harder than ever, to the neglect of even some health issues. While ISTJ men are the least likely to have a weight problem, weight and bad eating habits can plague ISTJ women more than some other types.

Among the many strengths of the ISTJ is the ability to act quickly and, very often, correctly. They have a propensity for beginning projects and staying with them through completion. This drive is aided and abetted by their dogged determination for covering all details and staying specific. It is the ISTJ who has given the workplace so many of the "scripts" by which we operate: "An idle mind is the devil's playground." "Waste not, want not." "Work as hard as you can, save as much as you can." "Hard work never hurt anyone." "Anything worth doing is worth doing well." "A penny saved is a penny earned." Clearly ISTJs work to live and live to work.

For ISTJs work comes first, then family and community responsibility. When all of this is in order, then it is okay to schedule some play. These are the compulsive types who "bring the office home" at the end of the day. If it's a family-owned business, it is expected that the entire family *will be* involved. There is no choice in this matter; if everyone contributes, everyone will benefit.

The ISTJ is often very calm and cool, even somewhat unexpressive or undemonstrative. This can be a strength in some situations, particularly stressful ones, when ISTJs appear rock-solid. This makes them more effective in many of life's emergencies, from operating rooms to battlefields. Indeed ISTJs predominate throughout the military, from enlisted personnel to general officers. While ISTJs themselves comprise only about 6 percent of the general population, they comprise about 30 percent of the U.S. armed forces. The ISTJ's four preferences are found overwhelmingly in the military: the combined army, navy, air force, and marines is 58 percent Introverted, 72 percent Sensing, 90 percent Thinking, and 80 percent Judging—ISTJ

If anyone invented the chain of command, it would probably be an ISTJ. Throughout the business world, whether a megacorporation or a mom-and-pop shop, they establish a structure and work it most effectively, expecting others to do likewise. When they are lower on the organizational ladder, when given an order, being Judgers, they may first complain, then obey by delivering the goods. Further up the ladder they give orders and expect obedience. If they don't get it, they are prone to take names and kick ass. They live by *shoulds*, and they impose them freely. They get the job done.

Unfortunately they sometimes get carried away. ISTJs can be the personification of compulsivity, driven by such things as deadlines and bottom lines without regard to employee motivation, satisfaction, or well-being. Striving for efficiency, they may instead produce a work force full of hostility, stress, and absenteeism. In the process other types can get weeded out, resulting in an even more ISTJ-oriented organization. The result is compulsivity to the nth degree.

ISTJs not only drive others to the brink, they can also inflict severe damage on themselves. This comes partly from their combined control and compulsiveness, which can lead to an attitude of "If you want it done right, do it yourself." This sets them up for long, lonely hours of doing everything—or at least doing the same thing over until it's right. In fact, more than any other type, ISTJs are capable of literally working themselves to death.

ISTJs also can get tripped up by their high need for privacy and their low need to express themselves. As a result others have trouble "reading" the ISTJ, sometimes creating serious communication gaps in an organization. Without saying a word, they may give off an aura of being impatient and even disapproving when that isn't necessarily the case. As a result there's an unwitting "show me" or "prove it" stance to the ISTJ's demeanor: *Show me* how it will be cost-effective; *prove to me* that you're right. The ISTJ's inexpressiveness often results in others feeling frustrated, flustered, or on the defensive. It may come as no surprise that ISTJs frequently make good loan officers.

Their inexpressiveness extends to giving praise, something they do with difficulty. It is expected that work be done in a timely fashion, neatly, and correctly. Therefore, believes the ISTJ, why would one praise what should be done? Your paycheck is praise enough—and if you last twenty years, we'll throw in a gold watch.

The ISTJ's no-frills style can lead to a workplace that is plain, austere, and conservative. Other types may find that it's not much fun to be working or spending time in such an environment. (Someone once quipped that ISTJ stands for "I Seldom Tell Jokes.") Such "amenities" as a comfortable chair, office decor, and extracurricular activities can often be seen by an ISTJ as a waste of time and money. In the long haul their quest for efficiency can sap employee morale and motivation.

The good news is that given good direction, ISTJs can make outstanding employees, managers, and leaders. That "good direction" usually comes in the form of a strict set of rules and regulations. ISTJs approach life much as a pilot approaches takeoff: no matter the task, to be effective, it is imperative to have a kind of "preflight checklist" giving specific, tangible instructions about what to do in a given situation. So, if good managers say, "Good morning" and "How are you?" every day to employees (even though it may seem unnecessary for productivity's sake to do so), once they are on the checklist, such greetings become something that are done over and over until they are an integral part of the ISTJ's management style.

While many organizational activities can be scripted and included on an ISTJ's checklist, not everything can. Most critically, what cannot be scripted includes those things having to do with pondering the big picture (iNtuition) and coping with interpersonal dynamics (Feeling). The big picture represents the unknown to the ISTJ, and the unknown is often more bad than good. Hence, too much "strategic planning" becomes a waste of time and things that managers do to avoid what needs to be done today. There won't be any future—or even a plan to implement—if someone doesn't pay today's bills or stay on top of the current crises. As a result the ISTJ can get blindsided by the unexpected, because the focus on today means that there is no contingency plan when surprises arise. So, it is far more effective to be doing something constructive and useful today than to wonder about tomorrow.

Subjective, Feeling-type decisions are another area in which the ISTJ can be found wanting. The entire world of interpersonal dynamics is difficult for this type since it is not predictable and can't be controlled. It is the epitome of the "soft" sciences, which are abhorrent to the ISTJ because they cannot be researched and measured quantitatively. As a result ISTJs would rather avoid, or even deny, the existence of seemingly "touchy-feely" situations, even though these could include such innocuous encounters as saying "Thanks for your help," discussing as a team some work project, or having a beer with the troops after quitting time. These things can actually frighten an ISTJ because they can include so many unknowns and a high risk of losing control. Even more frightening are genuine interpersonal situations—an upset employee, for example, or someone expressing frustrations with his or her job. A quivering lip or the possibility of a tear being shed can paralyze an ISTJ, who is afraid of losing control and feels totally incapable of managing such situations. Furthermore the ISTJ sees such behavior as inappropriate and unproductive, to say the least. Inevitably the ISTJ will react by tightening the control ("Stop that. Crying never solved anything") or simply denying the problem altogether ("Let's just forget this and get back to work").

Compounding all of this is the fact that it's inevitable that an ISTJ will end up managing and working with at least a few Feeling types. These individuals respond to a whole different array of motivations than the ISTJ—fun, harmony, happiness, personal fulfillment, and social responsibility, among others. The more ISTJs can understand and accept these differences, the more they can realize that they needn't control or deny such seemingly unacceptable behavior, the freer they will be to let others behave true to their own type, with greater productivity the inevitable result.

The same problems that confound ISTJs in the workplace can trip them up in the marketplace. Not understanding that half of the buying public is driven by such intangible things as appeal, looks, image, and just plain feeling good, ISTJs can create products that possess engineering perfection but lack marketability. Historically, great innovators have been plagued by this very dilemma: Henry Ford's Model T, which worked great but failed to keep up with fashions, is a classic example. From carpets to car parts, ISTJs can often overlook the personal appeal that the Feeling side of preferences brings to a situation. Fortunately, true to their type, ISTJs who fully understand this potential blind spot have the capacity to equip themselves to overcome it, either through greater self-awareness or by surrounding themselves with other types who can fill in this missing dimension. To an ISTJ this can be just one more aspect of life for them to manage effectively.

The unknown, the future, and the unplanned are all stress inducers for the ISTJ. With their high need for accountability, they can become very edgy, if not angry, if deadlines are being ignored in favor of last-minute, seemingly harebrained aspects of a project. Even relatively simple things can trigger stress. For example, if a meeting is scheduled to end at 4:00 and someone raises a new concern at 3:57, the ISTJ will likely experience a rise in adrenaline, pulse, and anger. Anything that will help the ISTJ enjoy sensory awareness—touch, smell, taste, and so on—without seeming too irresponsible can provide spurts of refreshment and stress reduction. For them, stopping and smelling the roses (or watering the office plants), while extremely difficult for them to do, is absolutely necessary for their good health.

ISTJs' excellence in completing tasks and organizing life gives them a natural edge as leaders at all levels of an organization. The various accountability and productivity demands of all organizations, from meeting deadlines to staying within budgets to achieving production goals, are natural areas in which ISTJs excel. In addition to the basic management of equipment and personnel, they are well suited for a variety of positions, including certified public accountants (who require a focused and objective attention to details, must meet strict deadlines, and usually work alone), surgeons (who must be singularly focused, work by the book, and not get overly involved with their patients), and police and detectives (who must stick to "just the facts," stay objective, and work within the strictures of the law).

ISFJ

Committed to Getting the Job Done

America. Motherhood. A Hot Lunch for Orphans. Each are interchangeable with *ISFJ*. Bound by fierce commitment, intense responsibility, and deep loyalty, the ISFJ is the embodiment of putting service above self in most aspects of their lives. Unless you've experienced this type, it's hard to believe that someone can be so dedicated and dutiful in so many aspects of his or her life. It is amazing how nobly they work behind the scenes, allowing many great things to happen and glory to be afforded to others. This is a direct result of the ISFJ's stringent personal sacrifice and their dependability.

Cautious, reserved, quiet, and inwardly oriented (Introversion), ISFJs are content to work quietly by themselves. Their perceptions of the world are realistic, grounded, and present-oriented (Sensing), and they use those facts and realities to make decisions that are interpersonally driven (Feeling). They prefer to live their daily lives in a structured, ordered, accountable manner (Judging).

ISFJs can become so wrapped up in serving others that they are soon taken for granted. It is such a noble pattern that many other types perceive them in disbelief, assuming there must be a catch somewhere. Or at least that the ISFJ is keeping score and will, some day or another, cash in his or her chips. But that's not the case. The ISFJs' mission and desire is to serve, and one of their great treats is to see someone they have helped succeed as a result of their benevolence.

The ISFJ female fits most of society's norms, including the martyristic suffering-servant image. While other types become protective of the ISFJ female or angry that she allows herself to be taken advantage of, very little actually happens in the workplace to change this situation. When gender issues surface at work—charges of inequitable salaries, for example, or inadequate maternity leave—they will most likely be raised by an iNtuitive-Feeler—male or female—or a Thinking female, much to the shock and amazement of the ISFJ female. She may even send signals that such provocative behavior by others is most inappropriate. As such the ISFJ female unwittingly serves as a pawn for the status quo. Though she may agree with certain dissenting points being voiced, she still believes that change should take place through the chain of command, not in opposition to it.

Such a commitment to duty and obedience can also be a problem for male ISFJs, especially if they have climbed the corporate ladder. They have probably done so by playing a more traditional male role during working hours, offering strength and tough-mindedness when needed. The ISFJ male must decide early on whether to give in to the Feeling-Judging side of his personality and exhibit a more nurturing demeanor, or play to more publicly accepted male expectations. Should he acquiesce to society's demands to be more Tarzan than Jane, given the ISFJ's natural caution about self-expression, the resulting turmoil can lead to ulcers, weight gain, or other stress-related problems.

Who would not want an ISFJ in the workplace? The qualities of being organized, pleasant, and a dependable team player is a manager's dream. One only needs to be around an ISFJ for a short while to realize how pleasant and quietly gracious they are. Like other Feeling types, ISFJs do not cope well with conflict, so when office strife arises, they prefer to take a blind eye or bury it deep within themselves in the hope that it will soon disappear.

Other types, especially Extraverted-iNtuitives, can become impatient with ISFJs in two areas. One is the somewhat slow, deliberate, methodical—some call it boring—way they approach specific tasks. Those types more prone to a seat-of-the-pants flamboyancy find the ISFJ's quiet, self-effacing dependability irritating at best. Equally troublesome to others is the way that ISFJs let people take advantage of them—their cheerful readiness to be helpful to anyone at any time. Others view this as the ISFJ's low self-esteem, but in fact it is the ISFJ's high sense of duty that keeps them so committed. Interestingly those who have a low tolerance for such blind loyalty don't necessarily stop taking advantage of the ISFJ's generosity; they only become impatient that the ISFJ allows it to happen.

ISFJs can have high expectations of themselves and others regarding rules, regulations, appropriate behavior, and a series of other *shoulds* and *oughts*. Breaking them or being disrespectful is a no-no, and if one reaps the ISFJ's scorn, then forgiveness can be very slow in coming. ISFJs are one of the backbones of the organization as well as a key part of its institutional memory. While other types may brainstorm the great ideas—from new products and programs to the next office party—little or any of it will happen without the deliberate, detailed follow-through of the ISFJ.

Once ISFJs befriend someone or become committed to a project, their patience is considerable. They will persevere to complete the task, notwithstanding overtime; setbacks in materials, dates, or personnel; and personally performing at any level necessary, from sweeping the floors to hosting a reception. Like other Js they may moan about all the work, but unlike Extraverts they will keep it mostly to themselves. As good Fs they are always willing to pitch in and make a sacrifice for the good of the organization. While this feeds into their perception as martyrs, for the ISFJ it is a self-fulfilling process.

Another strength of the ISFJ is their tolerance for detail and routine. They are motivated by established ways of accomplishing something and will work best when one expects them to do things "by the book." Likewise, when the ISFJ is in charge, he or she will expect subordinates to work within established rituals. If you follow the rules, says the ISFJ, you'll get it done and you'll reap rewards. If you break the rules, you'll be punished for the resulting failures. For the ISFJ this is a system that works.

The quiet support and affirmation generally associated with ISFJs is a powerful asset in the workplace. It is a gift to be able to affirm others—at work or wherever—ahead of oneself. To give credit where credit is due is expected and reasonable, but it is purely ISFJ to let others get credit for work you have largely done. If everyone benefits from what has been accomplished, and the workplace is better for it, that is reward enough, thinks the ISFJ. The ISFJ is the ultimate team player. Moreover, for the ISFJ any activity can be part of a team endeavor. So, an ISFJ nurse is part of a "healing team" whose goal is everyone's good health. ISFJ teachers are part of a "community-family team" whose goal is to raise children. ISFJ clergy are part of a "spiritual team" whose goal is to offer moral guidance. ISFJ clerical-support staff are part of a "management team" whose goal is to deliver a good product.

Their sense of duty and obligation can also become a liability for ISFJs. They can become so hooked on commitment that they almost become doormats for the rest of the organization. There are times when the ISFJs ought to be more assertive of their own personal needs, especially when others take advantage of them. If they are not careful, ISFJs can wear an invisible sign that says, "Here I am, take advantage of me." They would do themselves and others a service if they would work at being more vocal and direct about their own needs. However difficult, this is absolutely necessary.

Another weakness of ISFJs can be their inability to see the forest for the trees. They can get so caught up in the immediate service or need that they lose track of just about everything. Having attended to the crisis of the moment—whether an accounting problem or a person in need—they suddenly find themselves tired, drained, and quite irritable because there are still seven hours to go in the workday and they have spent all their energy. When ISFJs get overextended, they exhibit wide mood swings, becoming very disjointed and spacey, going quickly from fits of boisterousness to intense introspection.

Though it takes a great deal to strike the ire of an ISFJ, when that finally happens, it will come in the form of a stubborn, unforgiving, unbending way. Often this is followed with a flurry of anger that can include a laundry list of pent-up issues—about work, people, or anything else in range, regardless of whether it's related to this event or individual. Once that happens, there is little chance for recovery, and the response is totally disproportionate to the event at hand. Had the ISFJ tried to share some of these concerns all along, they would not have festered, allowing the ISFJ to deal directly with the problem at hand.

Notwithstanding these potential weaknesses, our institutions and organizations would simply not work so effectively were it not for ISFJs. They serve as role models and inspiration for so much of what society deems good and noble. That, coupled with their tenacity, is why life happens so beneficially for so many of us. Some ISFJ somewhere is working behind the scenes, putting things together that we can then have, use, and enjoy.

An Inspiring Leader and Follower

Wherever scholarly dependability is needed in the work-place, there's no better person to turn to than an INFJ. A popular human-services-oriented type, most of their energies, at work or at home, are directed toward bettering a condition, especially the human one. No one word does justice to the complexities of the human personality. However, the word *gentle* continues to come to mind when thinking of the INFJ.

The focus of the INFJ is inward, meditative, and reflective (Introversion), and their perception of life is to see it as filled with endless possibilities and meanings, usually in a big-picture context (iNtuition). These symbols and abstractions are translated through their subjective, interpersonal decision-making preference (Feeling), which in turn is acted out in a lifestyle that is structured, scheduled, and ordered (Judging). The INFJ's iNtuition is Introverted, and the Feeling-Judgments are more imposed on others. The combination is a rather rich and imaginative inner drive that reveals itself in the form of caring and concern for others—with just enough structure to be believable. They're not all talk; they deliver the goods.

Many of the INFJ's descriptors—gentle, caring, concerned, imaginative, interpersonal—are those typically seen as more female than male. As a result INFJ females fit most socially traditional female expectations; one exception might be the aura of mysticism that many INFJs possess. It is only as the INFJ female gets driven by her causes and concerns that she may be less than pliable and therefore more threatening to the male-dominated workplace. When this occurs, it can become compounded because as the male pushes for facts and objectivity (a typical Sensing-Thinking model), the INFJ female can appear less than grounded—but no less firmly committed. At such times the ST male pushes harder and harder, only to be stymied in the INFJ's rigid (Judging) but idealistic (iNtuitive-Feeling) issues. Still, INFJ women are respected for their intellectual acumen and are seen as generally soft, gentle, and caring at work.

In our society these same characteristics in males are problematic. INFJ males are confronted with a difficult situation: Their natural caring gentleness is threatening to others in the workplace, particularly other males. The INFJ's colleagues, superiors, and subordinates alike are prone to wonder, "Who is this person? Is he a man? A wimp? A guru? A flake?" The INFJ is aware of this paradox. He knows he is different from society's norm and he feels society's pressure to be tough and macho. That leaves him with inner turmoil and with jammed circuits in his body.

All INFJs are more likely than most other types to suffer illnesses of the stomach and lower colon. It is almost as if they are punishing themselves for being unable to reconcile the public's expectation of their gender with their natural preferences. This can apply to women as well, but in our clinical observations, we have seen this much more in men.

In most cases the solution to this situation probably is not medical. It begins with an awareness of the dilemma and a recognition that INFJs are naturally adept at meditation—anything from a discipline such as yoga to the simple opportunity for a few minutes' quiet reflection. INFJ males would do well to take advantage of this for a few moments each day, even at company expense, for some sort of a meditative release. Such a break allows them to continue to be productive and allows others to benefit from their special contributions.

Outside of the clergy, and perhaps private-practice psychology, it is not an easy lot to be an INFJ male at work. Their intense concern internalized can become a heavy daily burden. It can also set them up for a martyr complex ("I'm so concerned about Sam, but he doesn't even seem to hear, let alone appreciate, my concern. Poor me"), which serves no one effectively.

The INFJ's overall work style brings a good balance of schedule and accountability with an awareness of others' needs. INFJs are particularly reticent when it comes to conflict and often know ahead of anyone else when it is about to erupt. Their Introverted-iNtuitive-Feeling provides a radarlike perception that can serve as an early-warning system. Unfortunately this ability flies in the face of their intense fear of conflict. The result leaves them debilitated. They bury the trauma in their Introversion and hope that it will simply go away.

INFJs like neatness and order at work and prefer a setting of quiet congeniality, a place where each person can be affirmed for his or her contribution, each feels a sense of accomplishment, and all work harmoniously toward some common good. Such qualities are extremely valued in the teaching profession, helping students to think for themselves and to appreciate learning; of course in the faculty lounge between classes the process will continue. These same traits are equally valued in other professions, as INFJs share some friendly exchange, insight, or inspiration.

INFJs' strengths include their intellectual prowess, their personal idealism, and their general caring and concern for humanity. The combination of their four letters leads them to pursue the theoretical and accomplish most goals by which academic achievement is measured. Few people fully appreciate the rich inner life of the INFJ and how steeped it is in imaginative, creative, abstract ideas and concepts. The INFJ can easily spend an entire day just dreaming and envisioning. Such pursuit is its own reward, and to be allowed to do that—and to encourage others to do the same—is what life is all about for the INFJ. Consequently any task or event will always be the richer if he or she can first place it in some conceptual frame of reference that includes thinking it through thoroughly. INFJs' nonstop search for learning, self-growth, and development—and wishing the same for everyone else—makes them very reassuring to others and people worth emulating. Their keen insights and generally strong character are an inspiration to all.

Feeling types as a rule are idealists, and INFJs (along with their cousins, the INFPs) lead the pack. This is interesting, because while they are not given to rocking the boat, when an INFJ's ideals are on the line, it seems that he or she can take on any odds and win. So, if the issue is better pay for teachers, it will be the INFJs who will present it to the public in a formidable fashion. They may be less likely to walk the picket lines or make speeches, but they will no doubt be a driving force nonetheless. Suddenly this pliable, gentle, concerned INFJ can become a strong-willed determinist who faces a cause equipped with the intellectual foundation that can render opponents defenseless. Whatever the cause, you won't do badly having an INFJ on your side.

It is not unlike an INFJ to wonder why everyone isn't affirming, honest, and productive with one another. There is no need for war, believes the INFJ, only improved understanding. INFJs are the embodiment of the Golden Rule and the notion that, "Let there be peace on earth, and let it begin with me." That is what INFJs give, that is how they live, that's what they want from everyone, and as much as possible, that's where they put their energies, at work and at home. Though their Introversion may make them somewhat slow to give strokes freely and easily, they can nevertheless be counted upon to stand by those to whom they feel loyal.

Their interest in their fellow human beings is fierce, firm, and genuine. Life is generally a better place because INFJs have passed through it.

INFJs are not without their shortcomings. For example they have a tendency to become severely depressed when their ideals go unfulfilled. It is amazing how quickly the strength of the INFJs' rich inner imagination can turn to discouragement when others don't readily join or support their cause. What was inspiration now spirals ever inward toward self-punishment and deep-seated feelings of failure. Guilt becomes overriding and depression abounds. In such cases the INFJ tends to distort reality and to bury himself or herself in a barrage of despair, ending in, "No one gives a damn. How foolish of me to have thought otherwise."

Another INFJ weakness is their overpersonalization— almost fanatically so—of events that may not even concern them. Once an INFJ has taken on the cares and concerns of a situation, even a simple office issue can escalate into a major disaster. Once an INFJ has accepted the burden of a problem, it is now his or her total responsibility to save everyone and to make things right. Anything from an un-happy colleague to the needs of a Third World country can be translated by the INFJ as a personal failure. If this eager-ness to take on burdens is not checked, the feeling of failure only deepens, giving way to total self-deprecation and pun-ishment. The INFJ's resulting sense of worthlessness can permeate an entire organization.

A third weakness is the INFJ's propensity for making the simple complex, then becoming quite extreme in re-sponse—in short, making mountains out of molehills. They can become fanatics, responding to a situation in a manner totally disproportionate to what's demanded. A disagree-ment over a company's new lunchroom policy can quickly move from a simple dispute over rules and regulations into a crusade for ending hunger worldwide. Others are baffled at how this occurs. Moreover the INFJ will become rigid, with fits of anger followed by extreme withdrawal, making it almost impossible for others to reason with the INFJ.

When such behavior is minimized, the INFJ's contributions to the workplace can be significant. At their best they are imaginative and creative visionaries who are a source of inspiration to everyone. They are often the ones behind the scenes who make others look good, providing words, wit, and wisdom.

INTJ

Life's Independent Thinkers

When you consider how few INTJs there are in the U.S. population, it is astounding how much influence on corporate and academic life they have had. Their capacity for intellectual and conceptual clarity gives INTJs both vision and the will to see it through to completion—leadership qualities that are prized in our society. Perhaps more than any other type the INTJ has played a dramatic role in shaping American corporate culture.

INTJs view the world in terms of endless possibilities (iNtuition), to be manipulated, conceptualized, systematized, and translated through objective decisions (Thinking). These decisions are readily implemented because of their daily lifestyle of structure, schedule, and order (Judging). Their Introversion is the arena for developing their many ideas, which are usually many more than will ever be realized. However, the four preferences combine to convey confidence, stability, competence, intellectual insight, and self-assurance.

These four preferences are things that most people naturally rely on for strength and confidence, especially in the upper echelons of business. INTJs won't embarrass us by Extraverting when we least expect it, but will instead convey confidence that everything is in good hands. Rather than getting locked into details and specifics as a Sensor might, they translate the facts to a bigger picture to provide perspective. While subjectivity may be comforting to most people, it is objectivity that we associate with business. And our society operates and gives rewards based on a J time- and goal-oriented model. The INTJ packages these four qualities in a way that is not only generally appealing but is indeed relied upon for leadership and direction.

There are few things that a well-integrated INTJ cannot conquer with ease and grace. As a result these people are frequently elevated quickly in corporate circles and are looked to for exceptional leadership, which they deliver with aplomb. (We believe that this is the predominant type among Japan's corporate leaders. Their ability to take exist- ing ideas and improve each aspect of them, from design to production to marketing, has been a key factor in that nation's growing domination of world markets in the late twentieth century. One INTJ Japanese businessman even managed to adapt and improve upon the Myers-Briggs Type Indicator. Japan now has the second-largest population of Typewatchers in the world, after the United States.)

Though a single word cannot possibly describe any type, the word *independence* gives a thematic thrust to the overall drive of the INTJ. Clearly this is the force that motivates them. If they could, the INTJ would wish indepen- dence upon everyone. This drive for independence can conflict with the INTJ's need to control his or her immediate surroundings. So, colleagues and subordinates must recog- nize that while independence is the ultimate goal, it is to be meted out as the INTJ deems appropriate.

This apparent inconsistency can lead to some mixed messages. Verbal instructions that indicate flexibility and freedom—"Take as much time as you need and do it in whatever manner you think is best"—can have an underly- ing message of "Do it fast and do it right." The verbal message reflects the INTJ's Introverted-iNtuitive style, which is contemplative and open-ended. This can appear to conflict directly with their observable Thinking-Judging behavior, which seeks accountability and punctuality. But this is not inconsistent to the INTJ, whose *real* message is, "Every time you do it fast and right, you'll earn more flexibility and freedom."

As a natural conceptualizer the INTJ is the perfect "think-tank" specialist, intrigued by the future, stimulated with a rich imagination, and undergirded with good accountability. They are often looked to for solutions to complex problems. Consistent with their preferences, they provide direction and leadership with a creative flair. Someone once said that the most socially successful people are those who are independent (I), visionary (N), objective (T), and in control (J). Such individuals can be counted upon for anything; such a person is not always spraying you with his or her needs.

INTJ managers can be perpetual students. Always exploring and envisioning "what might be," their iNtuition is a reservoir of new techniques, programs, incentives, and directions for any system. Their propensity is to improve just about anything, even things that are working well; they'll fix it even if it ain't broke. It is an INTJ tendency to want to redesign IRS tax forms every April 15. This constant restlessness means that everything in the workplace is up for grabs. Constant evaluation and scrutiny—and perhaps revision—become driving forces on almost any project. Even if the mandate is to maintain the status quo, an INTJ won't be beyond trying to maintain the status quo with just a few improvements.

As with all Thinking types female INTJs face special challenges at work. Many of the traits described above—independence, objectivity, and control—fly in the face of traditional feminine models. Moreover the INTJ's need to challenge tradition and improve everything can cause friction in the male-dominated workplace. This conflict can lead to rejection by both genders: Males simply don't understand or know how to cope with the female INTJ's independence; other women see the INTJ female as arrogant, caring for no one but herself. Indeed INTJ women often have little patience for women who display traditional feminine characteristics.

Even more frustrating to some people is the INTJ female's tendency to be somewhat aloof: At work she is very carefully defined and extremely professional, guarding every word and action; private life is limited to a few chosen words and is kept quite separate from the office. Their guarded professionalism at work coupled with their seemingly asocial personal life wins them few allies among colleagues. Especially for INTJ females, it's lonely at the top.

The Typewatching maxim that one's strength maximized become a liability is certainly true for INTJs, although they would likely argue to the contrary. The INTJ's rich inner imagination, when left unchecked, can set them up for every form of counterproductivity: suspicion, distrust, and even paranoia. While everyone, especially Introverts, is capable of carrying on internal conversations involving others—who says what to whom and what happens next—INTJs in particular can carry such conversations to an extreme. Their rich reflectiveness can trick them into thinking that an imagined conversation really took place and that subsequent actions were taken. When this occurs, an INTJ's behavior can be marked with self-righteousness, arrogance, and a certain refusal to admit that he or she could be wrong or that the whole episode occurred only in his or her mind. Defensiveness, coupled with TJ self-confidence, can lead an INTJ to assume that others are not only untrustworthy but indeed are out to get them.

Such misplaced projection of the part of the INTJ can be very undermining to others and can leave staff or colleagues permanently wounded. Even then INTJs can be blind to their own destructiveness. Their tendency is to blame others for these circumstances. "If I'm good enough to get this far, then others, not I, must be wrong in their perception or judgment," they'll likely conclude.

Another possible weakness of INTJs is their tendency to give only intellectual assent to various management concepts. Team building, goal setting, and time management are all marvelous concepts—for others. Generally they would much rather write about, think about, or even improve upon any of these ideas than engage in the actual processes.

Like other iNtuitives the INTJ can become stressed from being bombarded by too many details. Their Introverted-iNtuitiveness would much rather imagine and speculate than put things into action. Consequently, when confronted with demands, especially those related to people's needs and seemingly trivial project details, the INTJ can become edgy, scattered, and even quite depressed. It's good for them to take a few moments out of each workday to allow time for reflection and contemplation. That will help to feed their inner inspirations and allow them to enjoy, even momentarily, the fantasy of "what could be" rather than "what is."

Such potential problems notwithstanding, INTJs can make a rich contribution to corporate culture. Their natural bent for achievement and excellence makes them successful in a variety of careers. Most anything to which an INTJ turns his or her energies can turn to success. They make excellent teachers, especially at the high school and college levels, because they bestow upon their students the gift of independent thinking. They are frequently good writers, administrators, researchers, and lawyers, especially managing partners.

ISTP

Just Do It

The ISTP is frequently misunderstood and often underestimated. Though very effective at most undertakings, his or her unorthodox way of accomplishing something, coupled with low visibility, can often lead to co-workers' wondering, to quote the people the Lone Ranger saved, "Who *was* that masked man?"

Indeed the Lone Ranger may be an appropriate symbol for ISTPs. They are frequently described with old clichés—"still water runs deep," or "a man of few words"—and they are difficult to read by others and slow to share in public. These qualities (Introversion), coupled with perceptions that are hands-on, tangible, grounded, and very much oriented in the present (Sensor), give the ISTP a somewhat cool demeanor. Decisions are typically objective, impersonal, and analytically driven (Thinking). The ISTP's daily lifestyle is spontaneous, flexible, and spur-of-the-moment (Perceiving), so that no matter what person or event comes along, the ISTP will be inclined to direct immediate attention, albeit privately, to the new set of circumstances.

Frequently ISTPs view the process of getting others involved as a waste of time. Participative management can be very difficult for this type. The ISTP is not opposed to it philosophically so much as psychically: Such a management style requires too much energy and effort to accomplish what to them is simple and obvious. It's not that they're lazy. Quite the contrary. It's just that they'd rather be *doing* than *planning*. They would rather be producing results than be bogged down in bureaucratic red tape. They would rather be putting out fires than designing fire drills. The tougher the problem and the quicker they can get to it, the better. ISTPs could probably embody the slogan of World War II's Seebees, a group of engineers that accomplished so much against so many odds: The difficult we do immediately. The impossible takes a little longer.

ISTP women, like other T women, have a particularly difficult problem with role identity and career fulfillment. Often when Introverted-Thinking is combined with Sensing-Perception one finds a loner who loves the tactile world of craftsmanship. The very word, reflective of generations past, can hardly be said in the female ("craftswoman") or androgynous ("craftsperson") forms. Indeed there is little historically that lends itself to affirming the ISTP woman. At the turn of the century, for example, the ISTP was typified by the tool-and-die maker, the self-taught engineer, the tinkerers who played with the early automobiles—racing them, refining them, constantly handling each part until it was as finely tuned as possible. The grease monkeys, the athletic perfectionists, the oil barons and drillers, the early pilots who flew unpredictable crafts over uncharted courses—all these typify the ISTP spirit. It is for them that the institutes of technology were born a century ago to sharpen the skills of this craft-oriented type. Little of the above comes close to describing the nurturing, gentle traits often ascribed to females. And when it comes to job choices, there is little here that is readily perceived by the public as "woman's work."

And yet there are many ISTP women who are capable, competent, and willing to work at many of these highly technical jobs. Over the last two decades they have increasingly embraced traditionally male occupations, from forest ranger and fire fighter to emergency room surgeon and special police. But all of these roles can leave the ISTP woman questioning her own gender identity while simultaneously alienating the males, who may see her as a "turf invader." The ISTP's disdain for routine and flair for the untried are uncharacteristic of women in this society and are generally not well received in a workplace environment bent on structure and schedule. When the ISTP female appears in a male-dominated role—and proves herself to be as competent as her male counterparts—she sets herself up for endless scorn. Doing "man's work," and doing it better, is not the way to be popular on the job in today's sexist world. It can also raise doubts within the ISTP herself: "Am I normal to like such work? Is there something wrong with me?" She has a need for constant reassurance that her femininity is not measured by or wrapped up in any particular vocation. Both men and women must understand that one's femininity (or masculinity) is not defined by one's job or competence.

ISTP women are more likely to see a job as genderless and be drawn by its special thrills or tangible and immediate rewards. But by breaking from societal norms, they find themselves in direct competition with their male colleagues. It is sad that when an ISTP woman excels at work, so far removed from traditional roles, it becomes major news, whether it is a woman who gets a court order to become a municipal fire fighter or a sports reporter who finds herself in a men's locker-room dispute. Such overdramatization, while perhaps encouraging to other ISTP women, tends to make the individual the exception instead of the norm for a considered section of the population. Furthermore, with the media involved, sides tend to be taken immediately—men versus women—and the real occupational desire and the potential contribution of the ISTP gets lost in the process.

Much as they disdain management theories, ISTPs are uncomfortable with management practice too. The ISTP's overall management style can be abrupt, direct, and often unorthodox. It's a let's-do-it-and-not-talk-about-it approach to motivating others. The problem of course is that many other types *need* to talk about it before doing it. (Extraverts may want to talk about it *ad nauseam*.) As such, when ISTPs climb the management ladder, it is only done so long as it seems to be an exciting game. As the game wears thin, so do ISTPs' patience; they will be ready to move on at the slightest provocation. If they stick to it, they'll eventually find some way to upset the applecart, if only for the thrill of it.

In a society that throws out and replaces rather than repairs—possessions, people, ideas, whatever—it is difficult to appreciate what skill, exactness, and perfectionism the ISTP brings to life. For the ISTP the naked eye is a perfect plumb, the ear is the instrument that tunes complex machinery into perfect harmony, the nose analyzes and interprets the various aromas for the florist, the chef, or the gardener. These are accomplishments of the senses, and to rely on some technical machinery for such expertise is to deny the special gifts of the ISTP.

A strength of the ISTP is the ability to self-start and to work independently. As we've said, they're better independent workers than team players. Their perfectionism combined with their personal integrity results in a job well done with minimal supervision. Generally projects that allow some flexibility of schedule are readily accomplished. They'll get the job done on time, but not necessarily on your schedule; they do not do well with PERT charts.

The ISTP's flexibility allows them to adapt easily to unscheduled events that may unglue a more structured type. As long as the ISTP can see the work progressing, interruptions are almost welcome because they keep things from becoming too dull or routine. Change Orders or Project Modification Sheets are frequently met with the response "No problem." This fits perfectly the ISTP model: flexibility grounded in common sense.

Still another strength of ISTPs is their ability to amass technical data without being burdened by the need to create outcomes, schedules, predictions, or any of the other results often demanded by the workplace. This makes them excellent research analysts, albeit somewhat slow to publish results. This is not in conflict with what we earlier described as the ISTP's need to do rather than to think or plan. In their endless gathering of data it is the doing—the pursuit of information—that is what's exciting; indeed the next steps—analyzing and processing the data—are activities that leave the ISTP cold. We have a colleague who has collected thousands of completed Myers-Briggs answer sheets. While he has scanned them and garnered some fascinating insights from them, he has done practically nothing with that information and finds little need to do so. (Other types would find this anathema: Extraverts would want the public recognition, iNtuitives would enjoy exploring the possibilities, Feelers would want to use the data to help others, and Judgers would want to wrap the project up and move on.)

The bugaboos of the ISTP at work can be summed up in three words: routine, administration, and paperwork. Such statements as "We've always done it that way," "We've never done this before," or "This is the way it should be done" are invitations for an ISTP to break the rules or bend the routine just for the thrill of it. While any of the Perceiving types can become bored with administration, ISTPs in particular have trouble seeing the need for such boring work. For the ISTP, files are where you put things you'll never use again, ledgers are for figures you'll never need again, and Day-Timers™ are where you keep data you never really want. "Life is easy," says the ISTP. "Live it one day at a time, and don't sweat the small stuff. Use your time and energy wisely today, and tomorrow will take care of itself." And what kind of paperwork do you possibly need to keep the world in tune—technically, artistically, and functionally? Paperwork, the ISTP believes, was conceived by someone who wants to keep others from getting things done.

```
┌─────────────────┐
│                 │
│                 │
│      ISFP       │
│                 │
│                 │
└─────────────────┘
```

Action Speaks Louder Than Words

The term *ISFP manager* is almost an oxymoron. Though a significant part of the work force, they are rarely positioned in a leadership spot and would much prefer a service-related position. Indeed they are not above passing up a promotion so that they can stay "where the action is." It's not that ISFPs aren't capable, although they do tend to be self-effacing. Indeed they possess some impressive natural skills for relating to all forms of life—plants, animals, and people.

Each of the four preferences feed each other in helping the ISFP relate to others rather than invading their space. The ISFP begins by focusing internally rather than externally (Introversion) and strives to be sure that his or her own internal world is in order. Their principal goal is not to reshape others so much as to define their own needs and concerns. The world itself is very tactile, immediate, and grounded (Sensing), and this is translated through the ISFP's subjective decision-making process (Feeling). They have a low need to come to closure about any of these things—Introversion, Sensing, and Feeling—preferring to stay open and experience all of it (Perceiving).

As a result it is this type more than any of the others whose style is to stand by another person (or plant or animal), with no intention to influence it, criticize it, or change it—perhaps not even to interact with it—only to be in its presence. Other types can hardly believe the ISFP's lack of intentions, let alone trust it. There must be some hidden motives, they believe. Surprisingly enough, there aren't. Live and let live, might be the motto of the ISFP.

ISFPs are generally very easygoing, low-key types with little need to influence those around them. They are so low key, in fact, that they can begin to question their own motivations, perhaps even wondering why they're not more given to controlling others and taking charge. Such questions can lead to large doses of self-doubt. Perceivers are generally prone to second-guessing their decisions, often wondering such things as, "If we waited just a bit longer, would things have turned out differently?" When you couple P with internal, here-and-now subjectivity (ISF), most of life becomes a series of what-if, let-it-alone, maybe-tomorrow-will-be-different experiences that leave the ISFP vulnerable to severe self-criticism. All of which is unfortunate because the natural, unobtrusive, accepting manner of the ISFP is not only a great strength—and much needed at all levels of organizational life—but it is also refreshing when encountered in the workplace.

Obviously, because of the preference for Feeling there will naturally be more female than male ISFPs. ISFP males are rarely given to the macho, tough-guy compensation often found among other Feeling male types. As a result they are quite easygoing and laid back, pleasant to be around and skilled at helping others cope with—or make the most of—the moment, whatever that is. Whether it's helping someone relax, serving as someone's sounding board, or providing an alternative to a sticky problem, ISFPs of both genders are at their best when others are in need.

Like other Fs the ISFP can get into guilt and self-punishment when a work situation goes awry. Even areas where they had no accountability whatsoever can become sources of overidentification, and undue energy can be spent in sympathizing with the underdog or the wronged, or even the guilty party.

Leadership, as we said earlier, tends to elude the ISFP. They can be cajoled into accepting leadership positions, but it is really not the best use of their talents. They can be capable leaders for short periods, but over the long-term, to be under the constant fire of deadlines and other pressures will be highly stressful to an ISFP, who would rather remain invisible and behind the scenes. If the position demands high accountability and high visibility, ISFPs will have to expend inordinate energy to rise to the task. Their natural talents lie in the service portion of a given job description. Service, in fact, is the cornerstone of ISFPs' motivation, and they are at their best when what they are doing has a significant service component to it.

Natural strengths of the ISFP in the workplace include supporting and helping others; finding alternatives to seemingly frozen projects or relationships; negotiating options to a problem in a way that everyone wins; troubleshooting difficult situations for more effective interpersonal communications; and, probably more than many other types, keeping people in touch with tangible, attainable goals. It's the ISFP who best helps us see the need to approach a project a bit at a time rather than being overwhelmed by the magnitude of the situation. Any dilemma can be conquered when subdivided into manageable parts.

People work best, believes the ISFP, when they are encouraged and helped rather than criticized. Consequently, when leading they do it by quietly supporting and working with their subordinates as well as their colleagues. Indeed they may have trouble delineating between themselves and those below them, setting themselves up to be taken advantage of. But this unaggressive management style can also build fierce loyalty among those of their department who appreciate the freedom to work at their own pace and in their own style. Support and affirmation from an ISFP often come in the form of nonverbal self-expression. When you work for an ISFP, you are more likely to receive praise in the form of a deed or an unpredicted gift than a verbal pat on the back. A bouquet, an afternoon off, a special unexpected privilege are all signs of an ISPF's approval. For those who need more overt, direct, and regular affirmation, the ISFP's style can leave them wanting.

A happy work team is a productive work team, believes the ISFP, so energy is better spent in making the environment pleasant in the assumption that productivity will follow. Any excuse for a break in the action—a cup of coffee with a colleague or a moment to listen to someone else's problems—helps to keep things interesting and themselves motivated. Likewise if enough time is not spent in creating a spontaneous environment, then not only can the ISFP become critical and depressed, but this can also become an excuse for low productivity and absenteeism.

Even more than other Perceiving types, follow-through and routine plague the ISFP. It's far more exciting to be working on a new or nonroutine project than just doing the same old thing. It's much more stimulating to respond to some emergency than to be in an appointed place at an appointed time doing the stated assignment. It's significantly more important to rescue some person or animal in need than to be at one's desk, completing whatever was started yesterday. As a result both boredom and listlessness hover over ISFPs and can be their undoing if they are not actively pushing things to completion.

Because of the dichotomy between service to others and shortness of attention, the ISFP can lose interest in high productivity. That is not their interest nor their arena, and they need not punish themselves for not playing the accountability game. Above all it would be helpful for them to avoid the stresses that such high-performance demands can impose on an individual. For the ISFP those stresses can lead to ill health, frustration, even severe depression. It's better for them to focus their energy toward helping others and giving their best to a particular situation, meeting the needs of the moment and let everything happen the way it will instead of beating themselves up for things they cannot control.

Often the more demanding types set the ISFP up to live or work on the wrong turf, then even join in helping the ISFP's self-flagellation. If an ISFP is a skilled bookkeeper, for example, others might encourage, even demand, that he or she strive for a CPA degree. But the ISFP may have little need for such ambitious achievements, being much more pleased to work responsibly where he or she is. In such a process the ISFP's contribution to the workplace can be lost, and the workplace becomes much less personal because of it. Because the ISFP is easygoing and harmonious, others are seemingly always "shaping them up" to be more like the mainstream or sending them somewhere—especially to therapy—to be "fixed." Even if the "fixing" is successful, what's lost in the process is the ISFP's unique contribution of support, encouragement, and self-enhancement, which most organizations so desperately need.

The ISFP is the type that can get things done, often unconventionally. And other types, especially Thinking-Judgers, find such unconventionality stressful. The ISFP is the type who quietly delivers the goods, knows the shortcuts through the complex bureaucracies, and can make others feel very affirmed and worthwhile in the process.

A severe dilemma in all of this, however, is that our system makes such demands for formal education and advanced degrees that the natural skills of the ISFP are rarely given a chance to be used. It is the ISFP at his or her best who embodies the humanistic ethic and who, when given the chance, quietly lives it. Deeds are always more fitting than words to the ISFP.

Professions such as teaching, especially grade school, clergy, any of the religious orders that involve service, nursing, paramedics, and clinical and educational psychology are all naturals for the ISFP. The bad news is that these careers frequently demand such prolonged academic training that few ISFPs can maintain interest long enough to succeed. In the nonprofessional work force one finds the

ISFP in the skilled crafts—butchers, bakers, and candlestick makers. Unfortunately it is just these skilled, hands-on crafts that are increasingly outmoded in today's high-tech world. All of which helps to create a bigger "supply" of ISFPs for a work world that doesn't seem to "demand" them.

While Saint Francis of Assisi and Mother Teresa are probably perfect role models for an ISFP, a contemporary model might be Charlie Brown, the "Peanuts" character. He assumes the role of baseball team manager, only to his constant distress and undoing. His Introversion won't let him even say hello to the little red-headed girl, and his Sensing-Perceiving side will risk everything to try to kick the football, despite the high probability of failure. His Feeling side—indeed his whole type—is personified by his classic line, "How could we lose when we were so sincere?"

```
┌─────────────────┐
│                 │
│                 │
│      INFP       │
│                 │
│                 │
└─────────────────┘
```

Making Life Kinder and Gentler

Whether leading or following, INFPs work best and are more productive when the effort reflects some ideal or service. Work performed for the sake of work, or meaningless routine, can render this type listless and perhaps even rebellious.

Clearly INFPs are best when whatever they're doing serves their personal values. However, if they can at least translate the work into some sort of meaning or human service, it may make something they don't want to do somewhat worthwhile. For example learning computer work for its own sake, while initially stimulating, will wear thin in no time. On the other hand the same work, if it can lead to a teaching or serving of others through computers, will be endlessly stimulating and satisfying.

For the INFP reflection and contemplation (Introversion) are coupled with a preference for abstract, futuristic, imaginative perception of the world (iNtuition). They make decisions subjectively, based upon personal values (Feeling), but such decisions are more directed toward keeping their own house in order than toward overtly controlling others. The INFP's day-to-day lifestyle is easygoing, flexible, and adaptive (Perceiving). All of which makes for a reserved but warm and gracious type who is frequently comfortable to let everyone "live and let live." It is only in the domain defined by their values that the INFP can become somewhat controlling. But that only happens when he or she feels something personally important has been invaded.

When INFPs are simply a part of the work force—as opposed to running it or being responsible for some part of it—it is only necessary that they find personal meaning in their work to be motivated. As their sphere of influence increases, so may accompanying controls. As a co-worker an INFP may stand by idly as you perform your job poorly. "It's none of my business, and you'll pay your own dues" is a typical INFP mind-set. But as a supervisor, or if your behavior has an impact on the INFP, he or she can indeed become quite (albeit somewhat subtly) controlling. Like other Perceiving types the INFP may not even be aware that you've stepped over that fuzzy boundary until it happens. Coupled with their Introversion, which impedes direct confrontation, it can make life a little frustrating for both parties: for you, because you were caught unaware of your misdeed; and for the INFP, who may have a reaction to the misdeed that is much more intense than is ever communicated and who may even be surprised by the suddenness and intensity of his or her own feelings. While it may seem out of character for this otherwise congenial and flexible type to become so rigid and unyielding, it's not out of character at all when one understands the unique nature of the INFP's four preferences.

In hard-charging executive positions the INFP is the exception rather than the rule: you'll find precious few INFPs as chief executive officers. However, when it happens, senior-ranking INFPs generally engender fierce loyalty among their subordinates. They usually do a good job of blending productivity with compassion for the work force. While the genuine respect others feel for an INFP superior may get in the way of specific disagreements, and while open conflict may be dramatically eschewed, those who work for INFPs enjoy the freedom to develop personally, receive generous affirmation, and have a ready, willing, and supportive ear for almost any idea. Even if you try and fail, as long as you haven't offended the INFP's personal values, he or she will affirm and encourage you for your effort.

If you do manage to offend the INFP's value system—and remember, no one may know of the offense until well after the fact—then forgiveness may be very slow, if ever, in coming. The situation is compounded because the INFP's Introverted-Feeling side may never forgive or forget. But their imaginative flexibility side—iNtuitive-Perceiving—will continue to give off accepting, easygoing, "It's okay" indications. For example, if it's an Extraverted-Judger who goofed and said, "I'm sorry," and the INFP responds typically ("It's okay, it was nothing"), then the EJ would naturally assume that the apology has been accepted and the matter is settled. But that may not be the case at all.

Though INFPs are underrepresented in the general U.S. population, there will statistically be more females than males simply because more females share the F preference. Where one finds INFPs in positions of power and control is in the realm of movements or institutions centered around social causes. One only need think of some cause—such as Mothers Against Drunk Driving, Women's Lib, the Myers-Briggs Type Indicator itself—in which one person was the driving force behind a cause, promoting something better for some group—and an INFP will inevitably be that person.

The male version of the INFP usually assumes leadership positions in an effort to merge his vision with some sense of accomplishment. When that happens, the INFP male will be a highly inspirational leader, though routine details can be a bore and can lead to his undoing. He may also get hooked into some more macho behaviors in an effort to compensate for the congenial, tenderhearted, softer male image others may see and criticize. He may take an unyielding position or a tough stance just to prove his mettle.

A disagreement or an opposing point of view can be stressful to any INFP. It can also give way to the dynamic discussed above, where apparent surface-level tolerance of the disagreement belies a very sharp judgment. INFP males and females, in their desire to let others develop and be independent, can often be torn between direct influence (because the issue is important to the INFP) and gentle persuasion (so that the person involved can feel he or she has influenced the end result). If this process is not carefully executed, it can be read by others as manipulation and deviousness on the INFP's part. The INFP's four-letter opposite, the ESTJ, is most likely to be the one to interpret such behavior this way and the one who will be most offended by it. An INFP manager once told us, "Once I have made up my mind to do something, my job as executive is to do it in such a way that the staff feels they have accomplished it."

When the workplace become too toxic or negative, the INFP can become restless or uneasy, falling into avoidance patterns typical of Feeling types. Tardiness, hypersensitivity, uncharacteristic mediocrity, and minimal effort are some of the behaviors that may begin to surface. All of this can grow into near-manic swings between sullenness and raging criticisms. The criticisms often carry previous baggage totally unrelated to the situation of the moment ("And that's not all. I've also had it up to here with . . .").

Such behavior is uncharacteristic for an INFP and indicates the presence of some stressor. If not checked early, the stress can fester, eventually escalating into bouts of ileitis and colitis, both of which are particularly prevalent in INFPs. Such problems can be minimized by offering INFPs a listening ear and encouraging them to talk through their issues. However, as Introverts they will find this difficult to do, however beneficial they may recognize it to be.

Because of their intellectual astuteness, competence, and idealism, INFPs do well in climbing the organizational ladder. In some ways it aids and abets their high need to provide service to others, but it can conflict with their equally high need for perfectionism. This can result in an overextension of self and tireless (often perceived as thankless by the INFP) efforts for the organization. This leads to severe self-criticism because, in the INFP's mind, there is never quite enough time or the job is never done quite right. As such they can become martyrs, cutting off meaningful dialogue with the very people who are attempting to help them—superiors, colleagues, and subordinates.

INFPs are probably at their best when they are enabling others and satisfying their own ideals. As their responsibilities increase, INFPs are inevitably promoted into positions that move them away from the matters of the heart at which they had been so successful. INFPs would be well advised to think twice about accepting a promotion that may offer ego gratification but may move them beyond those activities at which they excelled. A good example is the INFP pediatrician who gives up private practice to run a state or federally funded program in pediatrics, thinking it will benefit more children in need; however, the job ends up involving much more politics and administration than helping, skills at which INFPs are not adept. In moving away from hands-on caring for children and into a world of bureaucracy, the pediatrician is likely to end up with self-doubt, self-criticism, and unhappiness. If INFPs are going to broaden their service base, they must swallow the bitter pill and recognize when to quit, when to live with a product that is less than perfect, and when to recognize that others are not going to live up to or work according to their expectations.

INTP

Life's Conceptualizers

INTPs are free-spirited idea mills and absentminded professors, which makes them fun to be around, easily diverted, and a plethora of unending creativity. Their love of the abstract is sufficiently deep that it can lead them in the course of the working day through a maze of inventive and challenging programs, policies, products, and processes.

The INTP's source of energy and favorite turf is inward, reflective, contemplative thoughts (Introversion). Their perception of the world is conceptual, abstract, and random, with endless possibilities (iNtuition), which is used as the basis for objective, impersonal decisions that weigh carefully the cause and effect (Thinking). All of this is translated into a flexible, spontaneous, adaptable, easygoing lifestyle (Perceiving).

The INTPs' iNtuitive-Perceiving nature frequently leads them astray in the pursuit of new adventure, which can interfere with their need for time to be alone and to think. For the INTP it's hard to stay removed and reflective in one's internal world when the outer world is so full of ideas and possibilities. The INTP is a very heady, conceptual type, whose ideas can be pure genius. Sometimes these ideas get lost because INTPs tend to rework them continually and don't always share their latest thinking.

Both male and female INTPs face gender issues, albeit very different ones. The female INTP often finds herself between the proverbial rock and a hard place, in which society's traditional demands are juxtaposed with her natural preferences. For example, at one extreme INTPs can be somewhat independent, antiauthoritarian, argumentative, sometimes shy and socially awkward (depending on the strength of their Introversion), and not particularly given to most of society's customs and traditions. They are not against any of those traditions; it's just that in their absentmindedness they can often appear disrespectful of some basic social gesture or observance. Coupled with the Introverted-iNtuitive-Thinker's propensity for intellectual arrogance and impatience, you can imagine the trouble in which the INTP woman can find herself.

Generally, before any INTPs seek to engage someone on a particular subject, they will likely have done their homework. They do it for at least three reasons. First they would not want to appear incompetent. Second, "homework"—research, reading, getting one's ducks in a row—is something INTPs enjoy and do very well. Third, in such an engagement INTPs want to present an impressive point of view that reflects intellectual prowess. Though the INTP woman wants to excel at all of the above, none of this is perceived as "womanly" by others. The dilemma is compounded since the INTP woman appears intimidating and even condescending to others. In any intellectual engagement the INTP woman is likely to win her case, but may pay a price in the form of alienating others.

In a system that does not reward Introversion—and in fact is distrustful of it—the situation may be compounded when the Introvert is female. While it can be intimidating to encounter anyone who is intellectually astute, cool, and aloof, it is especially unnerving when the individual is female and appears more scientific and studied than soft and solicitous.

Male INTPs may have a somewhat easier go of it because being cool and aloof is more in line with expected male behavior. Yet being true to type can still cause problems. Their easygoingness and conceptual spaciness, for example, can put them at odds with the Thinking-Judging management style of most organizations. There's always some reprimand in order about the INTP being more grounded and less "out to lunch." "Stop daydreaming and get back to work!" and "I'd like to see you show a bit more respect for rules and regulations" are two common demands made of INTPs.

Other problems stem from their lack of social awareness. While all INTPs are uncomfortable socially, this is more pronounced among males; INTP women seem to get through social encounters somewhat more easily. INTPs may find themselves at odds with co-workers for their lack of enthusiasm for organizational parties and other social events. It's not that they don't want to attend these things—they may find them tolerable, maybe even enjoyable—but when the events continue for too long or, worse yet, don't include any deep or meaningful dialogue, the INTP sees them as a waste of time. So, INTPs would rather just keep on working, finding "meaningful dialogue" in their own inner thoughts. Both male and female INTPs may end up feeling guilty for having forsaken their social duty in favor of their own Introverted needs, perhaps not having satisfied either. While feeling true to themselves, they may be thinking, "I've screwed up again."

At work INTPs are sources of ideas and inspiration who often work most effectively on their own. They are generally creative and given both to high energy and to occasional bursts of fun. They are not beyond dropping everything to join in on some new project or brainstorming session. They can be somewhat frustrating if one expects too much detail or attention to the bottom line. Time constraints are not top priorities for INTPs, and they may find themselves stretching deadlines from time to time. All life—including work—is an intellectual challenge to the INTP. Things need to be thought through thoroughly before being undertaken, and then perhaps thought through one more time. INTPs prefer that words and arguments be formed with clarity and precision. They have little patience for those who talk out of both sides of their mouth, or who make small talk, or who reflect theoretical inconsistency—being both in favor of capital punishment and against war, for example. Such inconsistencies, when encountered in a dialogue, may bring forth an immediate—and very surprising—eruption from the INTP.

INTPs are easy to work for and with and enjoy banter, independent thinking, and especially self-directed projects. All life is learning for iNtuitive-Thinkers in general, and the INTP embodies this most completely. Therefore anything that can develop one's intellectual awareness has some value. From hands-on mechanics to proposal writing, it's one opportunity after another to learn, improve, and grow. Such drive is behind most of the efforts an INTP directs toward anything.

One of the strengths of the INTP is a penchant for independent thinking, both in themselves and in others. To be able to develop something from scratch and think it through from beginning to end by oneself is a sign of real maturity. To command ideas logically and consistently is a work of art. The great theories of all time, from relativity to personality, evolution to thermodynamics, Parkinson's law to Murphy's law, probably had their incubation in the mind of an INTP. Even if your idea is harebrained, seemingly impossible, or even totally wrong, if in the process of developing it you have reflected good logic and verbal expression, then it is worthy of being listened to, according to the INTP. Moreover, in doing so you will gain the respect, perhaps even the friendship, of the INTP. However, the closer a friend you are, the greater the likelihood that your intellectual chain will be yanked by the INTP, because friendship will probably be defined as a mandate to challenge each other intellectually.

A second strength of INTPs is their clarity of thought and word, which accompanies most of what they do. INTPs are the natural writers and editors of life, who paint pictures with words. Their capacity to say exactly what's on their minds and to help others do so is a talent not readily matched by other types. The mind of an INTP is a steel trap, always tracking a conversation and restructuring it into perfect expressions. They can often repeat exactly what another person has said, even months later. Should one try to fend them off with an idle promise—"We'll talk about it later"—the INTP will undoubtedly be back "later," reminding the individual of his or her promise.

Still another strength of INTPs is their vision and enthusiasm for whatever is being undertaken. Sometimes their Introversion may block them from expressing all of what is going on inside them about a particular issue. However, they can usually take the general thoughts expressed by others and translate them into an inspiration and vision that motivates others. It is a real talent to see the ordinary for what it is. It is the gift of the INTP to add to the ordinary so that it becomes extraordinary. Day-to-day jobs become far more fulfilling when they are reframed by INTPs as integral parts of an organization's mission. If INTPs are given a moment to get their thoughts in order, their encapsulation may well be artfully stated. An INTP may view this process as natural; to others it's seen as "inner vision."

Perhaps the first and most serious shortcoming of INTPs is a direct result of their strength in the extreme: a failure to translate their rich inner concepts into meaningful action. It is not uncommon for an INTP to perform a job from beginning to end—but only in his or her mind. Whether assigned to write a request for a proposal or design a heater valve, the INTP will start by gathering all the data necessary to do the job—reading, listening, investigating, or questioning others. But the next step—translating this research into a report, drawing, or plan—may never actually happen. The INTP may well have thought it through thoroughly, and in the process even become excited about it, and then, having *thought* it through to completion, can safely lay the matter to rest. Moreover he or she will lose interest in any further pursuit of it, having likely moved on to some new project. Clearly this lack of follow-through can be extremely frustrating to those who were counting on the INTP's tangible results. For their part INTPs can get frustrated, too, knowing that the job is incomplete, but having little or no motivation to complete it.

Another INTP weakness is their social awkwardness. The INTP can exhibit wide swings, from genuine interest in a few special people to near total disdain for just about everyone else; INTPs may even be aware that this is happening. At times their keen interest in intellectual pursuits may draw them to one or more individuals, but such bonds can be easily broken should the intellectual focus move on to others. When confronted about their apparent fickleness, the INTP will likely deny it, act surprised, and promise to make amends, but it is unlikely that anything different will happen. It's simply part of being an INTP to gravitate to where the intellectual action is.

A third weakness of INTPs can be their low grasp of reality. Like other iNtuitives, and especially iNtuitive-Per-ceivers, INTPs can become very removed from the practical and realistic side of life. As a result deadlines get stretched, half-truths get told, and they can appear variously rigid or flaky when it comes to dealing with specifics. Moreover their behavior can become anything from loud and obnox-ious to pensive and withdrawn. Such behavior will become more pronounced as the INTP is increasingly under the gun to translate his or her rich mental ideas into tangible results.

The very intellectual basis of most of our life would not exist were it not for the INTP. Whether as teachers of higher education, scientists, editors, or computer programmers, they are the architects of our ideas. INTPs provide the conceptual framework by which manuals, organizational procedures, and even work assignments are translated and put into action.

ESTP

Making the Most of the Moment

The ESTP is a somewhat risk-taking, entrepreneurial, give-it-a-go person, a type with a real flair for most things. The ESTP has a fly-by-the-seat-of-the-pants attitude and is pleased to have everyone know about it. With a basic built-in restlessness, these are the hyperactive "doers," who like to keep their hands in a variety of pots, churning as much as they can to keep everyone on their toes and to keep life exciting.

ESTPs prefer to scan the external world of people, things, and action (Extraversion). They perceive the world in a hands-on, grounded fashion (Sensing), which they use as the basis for objective and impersonal cause-and-effect-based decisions (Thinking). All of this is constantly and immediately translated through a lifestyle that is spontaneous, flexible, and responsive to whatever happens (Perceiving). As a result of being so grounded and so Extraverted, ESTPs tend to be up-front and "out there" about life, capitalizing on each moment—because that's all one can be sure of. You only go around once in life, the ESTP believes, and it is incumbent on each individual to make the most of it.

For example, ESTPs can be so wrapped up in the moment that they can tell a story, overload it with exciting and colorful details, keep everyone in stitches, and have no point whatsoever. Clearly this can be extremely frustrating to those hanging on every word.

The nonconforming nature of ESTPs can make life especially difficult for females of this type. Like other Thinking women, they can become caught in the tension between social expectations and demands (to be nurturing and interpersonally sensitive) and their natural preferences (to be objective and remain detached from personal involvement). As a result, ESTP females can be quite rebellious, further exacerbating their gender ambiguity in the eyes of most sexist work forces. The combination of Sensing and Thinking—hands-on, tangible objectivity—is, by itself, somewhat at odds with expectations of what is "feminine" in our society. It is a straightforward, direct, nonpersonal approach to life. If the ESTP female is capable and effective in living her preferences, then she is apt to work in isolation, shunned by women who may be jealous of her ability to remain objective or by those who simply don't understand her. Men, for their part, find ESTP women's direct, pragmatic approach to life totally incomprehensible. Being a direct, witty, competent, and somewhat risk-taking female, no matter how refreshing, can leave old-fashioned colleagues aghast.

Like other Thinking types, ESTPs separate work and home, public and private, personal and impersonal, and everything else. If the ESTP female can accept these separations, she will likely affirm that she is no less feminine and that her contribution to the workplace can be significant. Still, she will be faced with the challenge of convincing others that her competency and her femininity can coexist. But this convincing will be best accomplished when starting from a position of self-confidence.

Male ESTPs have a somewhat easier situation—but only "somewhat," because their restlessness, love of the moment, and "fly-now-pay-later" lifestyle can cause them trouble when dealing with the structured, deadline-oriented, follow-through, focused workplace. So, while it may be more acceptable for males to be ESTP, it is still a type that will receive inordinate pressure to conform to the overall organizational type. ESTP males will resent such pressures and may react with disdain and rebellion.

The nonconforming nature of both male and female ESTPs often results in their prematurely tiring of the structured workplace, sticking around only long enough to master some skill. Ultimately, in their impatience, if they have not yet reached retirement, they will take their skill from job to job or engage in some form of independent work, either of which will offer the ESTP more immediate rewards.

The ESTP's overall work style is a potpourri of many things, largely driven by whatever works for the moment. Given the right incentives or deadlines, they may dig in and be both productive and dynamic. When the pace slows or the incentives disappear, it may be time to put up one's feet and shoot the breeze with colleagues. Rarely are they restrained by procedures or protocol. The sum total of this is unpredictability: When an ESTP is around, expect a spontaneous argument or a sudden burst of enthusiasm that leads the rest of the organization into some new adventure. Such apparent leadership notwithstanding, don't look to an ESTP for direction; they are less likely to take charge than to get wholeheartedly behind others' programs.

ESTPs are masters at getting to the heart of matters. Don't try to baffle an ESTP with flowery ideas and words; they not only see through it immediately, but your credibility will be lost with your own eloquence. Getting on with things—giving something a try, even a less-than-perfect idea—is better than debating it endlessly or studying it into submission. Doing something is always better than doing nothing—that's the Sensor's motto—and if you're a Perceiver, you can always change horses in midstream if things aren't going well. No matter that you didn't follow rules and regulations. If you get it done, the mere accomplishment will mend any people or policies that got bent out of shape along the way. For the ESTP tomorrow is a new day, and most of today's stuff will already be passé or irrelevant. As a result of this devil-may-care attitude, ESTPs are usually controversial leaders or workers.

One of the significant contributions of ESTPs to the workplace is their appreciation of the present moment. If we learn anything from SPs generally, and ESTPs most of all, it's that the only moment we can be sure of is the present one. Guilt over the past won't undo what has been done, and fear or even anticipation of the future is fruitless. ESTPs believe that focusing guilt, fear, or other such emotions upon the past or future only tends to make us less effective in the present. Get what you can and move on. For the ESTP, you work hard, and when it's time, you play hard. Don't bother with work that is intended to fulfill some long-range goal or requirement; that's all a waste. If the present is less than satisfying, don't avoid it or wish it away—change it now.

A second contribution of ESTPs is their ability to bring options to immediate situations and to move beyond the routines that might otherwise stifle productivity. For the ESTP all life is an option, and if your bent is to try almost anything once, something good is bound to come of it. Everything is negotiable, and there are alternatives to whatever is hindering a particular situation or action. So try, and try again. The trying not only gives you something to do, but it will inevitably create other options.

A third strength of ESTPs is the grounded pragmatism that surrounds them in the workplace. Working one project at a time is akin to living one day at a time, and that's where one focuses the energy of the organization. The ESTP has a sense of precision and attention to detail that is profound and can be very helpful when teamed up with another type whose absence of detail could stymie the project. ESTPs' social gregariousness makes them generally good team players and, as such, quite willing to be sure the specifics of a job are covered.

It's this same live-for-the-moment attitude that can engender ESTPs with a laissez-faire mind-set toward dependability and direction. Just when one is counting on them, they can be "somewhere else," either physically or mentally. It's a classic ESTP excuse to say, "I really intended to be here to help, but at the last minute . . ." As a last-minute type, "last minutes" become excuses for ESTPs to be anywhere other than where one expects them to be. Such apparent flakiness is not only frustrating to more structured types, but it can be downright disastrous to productivity.

Another weakness is the ESTP's proclivity for getting lost in the details of the moment. Their love of facts and figures can lead them to gather information for information's sake, ultimately inundating everyone with data for which there is no meaning or purpose. Thus, when a colleague or superior is seeking results, the ESTP's response could be, "I'm working on it" or "What's your hurry?"—both of which may be accurate albeit unhelpful. At their worst ESTPs can get so wrapped up in details that it can become difficult for them to sort out what's necessary to complete a project.

A third weakness of ESTPs is their highly visible restlessness when it comes to routines and other mundane details of life. You can tell in a second whether ESTPs are bored with something; they wear their restlessness and impatience on their proverbial sleeves. One can see how such impulsive behavior carries with it a win-big-or-lose-big price tag, with very little in between. Feeling types are apt to personalize this impatience, assuming it's their own problem, not the ESTP's. Other Thinking types tend to dismiss ESTPs variously as hyperactive, immature, or someone who needs their hindquarters kicked for their own good. Clearly the ESTP would be wise to attempt to lengthen his or her attention span. Similarly other types would be wise to try to help the ESTP see that routines, even at their worst, are necessary evils; at best they can become a challenging and productive way for the ESTP to move through the day.

Let's Make Work Fun

ESFPs love a surprise and are a surprise. It takes little imagination to appreciate some of the challenges and opportunities this type encounters in the relatively rigid workplace. Effervescent and exciting, free-spirited and fun-loving, nervy and nonconforming, ESFPs bring a breath of fresh air to any situation. Unfortunately their free spirit can also be a source of frustration to others and even themselves. Like most Perceiving types, for whom turning work into fun is an ongoing challenge, the ESFP is the embodiment of fun. That's what life is all about. So much a part of the ESFP is this fun dynamic that when something unpleasant cannot be converted to fun, or cannot be avoided completely, then it is time to simply drop the subject and move on to something different. For an ESFP, if you can't enjoy the fun, then you should at least enjoy the bliss of ignorance.

Each of the ESFP's preferences spell fun. These people are outgoing, socially gregarious, and interactive (Extraversion) and prefer to perceive the world very realistically, tangibly, and in the here and now (Sensing). These perceptions are all decided upon very subjectively, based upon the interpersonal impact each decision will have on others (Feeling). All of which is translated through a flexible, spontaneous, easygoing lifestyle (Perceiving).

Such a combination makes for a quick and ready wit, sometimes rather pointed and direct, but always out there for all to see, hear, and experience. Failure to understand this upbeat repartee can lead other types to misunderstand the ESFP and perceive them as either very superficial or coquettish or both. Such misunderstandings, when they occur, not only are harmful to the organization but also belie the real social breadth and interpersonal awareness that the ESFP contributes.

Gender issues for ESFPs affect both males and females. For males, it is the Feeling decision-making preference that can cause them to be seen as too soft-hearted to be a "man's man." But they can compensate easily by occasionally talking tough or dropping a little profanity into the conversation. However, they must still prove that they are capable of completing assignments and following through on whatever project is at hand. While all Perceivers can be plagued with this failure to follow through, for the ESFP male it can make others suspicious of his competencies. In general, ESFP males rise high within organizations and are frequently well liked by their peers, assuming their quick wits and blunt remarks don't alienate others along the way.

Female ESFPs are often subjected to a very negative stereotype due to the combination of a flexible public appearance (Extraverted-Perception) and their tendency to be literal and obliging (Sensing-Feeling). The result is that they exhibit some of the characteristics of a Gracie Allen or an Edith Bunker: flighty, airheaded, dizzy, or bubbly. It's not that they're dingbats; indeed many are extremely intelligent. It's just that their undaunted literalism can make them seem out of touch. (Gracie Allen, when asked "What kind of book are you reading?" would likely answer, "A paperback, silly. Anyone can see that"). Others often react to such responses with quick, personal judgments, missing the richness, capabilities, and keen social awareness that ESFPs bring to any situation.

The overall work style of the ESFP is marked with high energy and jovial interaction. There really is never a dull moment whenever an ESFP is present. They may not always be around when needed, they may not always be as timely as others might like, they may be overextended with too many irons in the fire (at least by some other types' standards), but they do accomplish what needs to be done. They can be as effective as they are pleasant to have around. In addition they will keep the office social calendar in shape—birthday parties, hails and farewells, or any other recognitions are capably attended to, along with the other demands the job may entail. (But not necessarily all of them: Their scattered nature may lead them to miss something important, from forgetting to bring napkins to failing to turn on the coffee maker.)

As fast as they move and as hyperactive as they appear, one would think that the ESFP would stay skinny burning up all that energy. But like their first cousin, the ENFP, both ESFP males and females can have a lifelong struggle with weight control. The combination of their preferences leads them to eat when they are happy, when they are sad, when someone new walks into the room, and whenever.

One strength the ESFP brings to the workplace is the ability to keep many projects moving at once. They motivate others when necessary, they freely pitch in and work side by side with any level of the work force, they have time to listen to others' personal needs—all the while keeping the overall goals and deadlines in perspective. All of this is accomplished in a very pleasant, flexible, and accepting atmosphere. Emergencies, however large or small, are viewed by ESFPs as welcome relief, not as intrusions. A busy day with a lot of variety—and maybe a few things left unfinished—is a great day and a real motivation to be back even earlier tomorrow. A spontaneous break, or a scheduled one, is an occasion to get caught up on office scuttlebutt, and all of this combines to make the time pass quickly and productively. Working with or for an ESFP is rarely dull—and usually a great deal of fun.

Another strength of ESFPs is their ability to let others be different and to work at an individual pace. Each of their four preferences—E, S, F, and P—lend themselves to an optimal awareness of the present moment and how unique and significant each person is at that moment. Consequently, if someone needs structure, the ESFP can help that person bring order to chaos, and by means of their chameleonlike nature, even become structured, too, if appropriate. They can affirm each person's efforts and are usually aware of how much may be going on behind the scenes, without necessarily becoming embroiled in it.

In bureaucracies or large organizations, they are particularly capable of working the system for the good of the people involved. For example, we knew a government employee who needed travel money late one Friday afternoon. Getting money that quickly and late in the week was considered virtually hopeless. Yet an ESFP colleague came through with the cash. Any ESFP would much rather accept such a challenge than stay working at a desk. With their friends all through the organization, and their ability to see ways and means around the various rules and regulations, ESFPs can in no time deliver the goods, no matter what the odds. No questions asked, the job is completed. Only a simple "Thank you" is required.

A final strength of the ESFP is their tempering perspective when deadlines become stressful. While other types may see the ESFP as irresponsible about deadlines and demands, as pressures close in, it is the ESFP, like no other type, who can identify with the frustrations, and perhaps the feelings of failure, and can say the right word or do the right thing to relieve tension and keep impending doom at bay. Rarely does an ESFP sit around feeling sorry for what's happened. He or she will face it, have some appropriate amount of guilt, then move on. Auntie Mame's "We need a little Christmas" in the middle of total financial ruin is a classic illustration of how ESFPs move themselves and others from life's tragedies to life's triumphs.

Like the other types, ESFPs also have their downsides,

and one of them is overextension. While they may work miracles in keeping so many balls in the air, it is easy for them to overcommit and run themselves into the ground. Once the process starts, the fatigue that accompanies such a situation can give way to despair, distrust, doom, and gloom. Such behaviors often grow out of ESFPs' failure to pace themselves, and with the inundation comes the misery.

Another shortcoming of ESFPs is their disdain for routine and their disrespect for structure and order. As a result they may never be where you want them to be, when you want them to be there. Though they may have a reasonable excuse for their absence or tardiness, it may have detrimental effects in the long run. Perceivers generally, and especially ESFPs, have trouble recognizing that routines are a fact of life. By simply ignoring them in favor of whatever is happening at the moment, the ESFP can be an irritant at best, an obstruction at worst.

Perhaps another downside is their weakness in grasping the long-term consequences of their actions. Because they are so grounded in the moment, ESFPs often do not see the impact their behavior, decisions, or actions may have on the big picture. As a result the consequences of something so simple as a whimsical flirtation or an offhand remark may be far more serious than the ESFP could ever have imagined. The off-putting was never intended, but it nonetheless remains an albatross to everyone involved.

A third drawback of ESFPs is that their never-ending quest for fun may not be welcomed in a workplace that sees profit and productivity as serious business. Indeed for many companies, *workplace fun* is an oxymoron; fun is what you're supposed to have at home or at the company's annual picnic. As a result some colleagues and superiors can hardly cope with the notion that fun may be good for morale and productivity. They may simply ignore the ESFP's overtures. More often than not, however, they invoke scathing judgments about the ESFP's behavior. For the ESFP, good intentions can quickly turn sour.

Such stumbling blocks aside, ESFPs are naturals in the

human services. They make excellent trainers, educators—especially elementary-level—religious leaders, sellers of almost anything, and athletic players and coaches. In these and other endeavors co-workers appreciate how effectively ESFPs accomplish what they do and readily begin to rely upon ESFPs to bring a special dimension of play to work, giving the workplace a little extra zip.

ENFP

People Are the Product

One doesn't typically consider the ENFP's characteristics—effervescence, enthusiasm, and spontaneity—to be those of top corporate managers, but the fact is ENFPs do very well in executive roles. At their best they bring a refreshing alternative style to top management and decision making.

A zest for life combined with social gregariousness (Extraversion) is linked with endless possibilities and alternatives (iNtuition) which ENFPs apply to a host of interpersonal encounters (Feeling) while always working their day-to-day events so as to maximize their options (Perceiving). Like their first cousins, the ENTPs, they can exhibit wide mood swings—almost within the same moment—and probably experience higher "highs" and lower "lows" in the process. Nevertheless they tend to bring enthusiasm and energy to most activities, which can be highly contagious, especially to those they lead. As they do with most things, their tendency is to convert managerial tasks to some sort of a grand game plan, then play it to the max, relying on their persuasiveness and creativity to keep people motivated.

The problem is that ENFPs can be so skilled at "flying by the seat of their pants" and doing a host of different things fairly easily—sometimes all at the same time—that they can neglect to make advance preparations. As a result, on any given occasion an ENFP can be found saying, "This is exciting, but I wish I had been a little better prepared," or "With a little planning, it would have gone that much better."

Though there are more female ENFPs than males, when it comes to promotions, it is the males who tend to rise to higher positions. This is a reflection not so much on the females as on the male-dominated Sensing-Thinking-Judging leaders who are doing the promoting. This can create some special problems. For example, because all ENFPs tend to be caring, empathic souls, their warmth can be mistaken as flirting or even worse, when this is generally not intended. With male ENFPs in higher positions, it sets up a dynamic in which their female underlings may become anything from flattered to resentful. What starts out as a natural warmth or affirmation can, at a moment's notice, turn quickly into a misunderstood innuendo, perhaps even charges of sexism or harassment.

Ironically, in their attempt to circumvent such scenarios, and because they are so readily adaptable, male ENFPs sometimes adopt a pseudo-ISTJ persona in order to project an image of toughness and masculinity. In the process they lose twice: Not only is their attempt to be something they're not less than successful, they cover up or deny their natural skills.

The female ENFP, too, has her problems. If she gives in to her natural ENFP tendencies, she may quickly become labeled "fluffy" or an "airhead," which may be far from the truth, her spontaneous and gregarious behavior notwithstanding. While such workplace qualities as warmth and empathy may be acceptable in males, they may not be in females. Her attempts to compensate by behaving in a more abrasive, guarded way fare no better.

ENFPs' ability to empower others is one of their most impressive contributions to the workplace. Unlike the control-obsessed Thinking-Judgers, ENFPs more easily encourage freedom and independence. In their persuasiveness they can easily accomplish the basic manager's goal of "getting work done through others" and at the same time make those "others" feel vital and useful in the process. Certainly there are some areas of work where they have some need to feel in charge—the specific areas may be different for each person—but as a general rule they are a reasonably nontoxic presence that gets thrilled about and revels in others' accomplishments. In the process there will be no hesitation from the ENFP in giving credit where credit is due. This can be inspirational, to say the least. Inspiration, rather than control, is key to the ENFP's management style.

Another great asset of ENFPs is their ability to generate options. It's always more exciting to engage in several projects at a time and to have more than one way to accomplish any one of them. Like the other EPs, this is an idea person who loves to upset the proverbial applecart and come up with new ways of coping with boring routines and slow-moving projects. Indeed it's often more exciting to generate alternatives than to complete the task at hand.

Still another asset is the ENFP's people skills. As a rule ENFPs give strokes freely and are responsive to other people's needs. They can generally find time to pause and help, affirm, listen, or do whatever else is needed to get someone unstuck and back into the swing of things. They tend to feel loyal to those who are responsive to their own enthusiastic way of relating, which in turn engenders more loyalty throughout the system.

For the ENFP stress generally comes in the form of those areas of their lives, private and professional, that cannot be converted into play or fun. As a task or responsibility drags on and its mantle becomes increasingly routine, the ENFP can become more pensive, moody, and even rigid. The more rigidity is demanded of the ENFP, the more rigid he or she may become, giving way to behaviors quite removed from his or her normal enthusiasm and effervescence. Filling out income tax forms, paying bills, working too much alone, or being compelled to meet specific deadlines are the kinds of tasks that set the ENFP up for stress and, in doing so, make them quite stressful to be around. Interpersonal conflicts and other "people issues" can all be distorted when the ENFP is stressed and can lead to wide behavioral swings by the ENFP. Such behavior has a tendency to spread quickly among others.

Those who must confront such behavior would do well to check the sort of tasks or work that is problematic for the ENFP. It is important to help the ENFP see that it is okay to work in fits and starts rather than according to some schedule. It would be even better if the task could be done collaboratively. Talking through the tax form is better for the ENFP than doing it alone. Generally an ENFP's stress is reduced by engaging others, even competitively. It helps them to attack stressful situations by creating a grand scheme growing out of whatever inspiration strikes them. Physical exercise, mental activities, and any of the meditative experiences are especially helpful to ENFPs, particularly when couched in the context of meaningful relationships.

A happy work environment is very important to an ENFP, and without it he or she can waste a great deal of company time on the wrong issues. Their natural ability to identify with others can mire them in unconstructive bitching sessions. Alternatively they can respond to a stressful workplace through avoidance—avoiding issues, certain tasks or people, perhaps even avoiding coming to work. In whatever fashion, it is an ENFP trait to become absorbed, perhaps even obsessed, with others' personal problems.

Though quite productive when allowed to work by themselves, those dependent on an ENFP can become frustrated by the ENFP's poor ability to manage time, work flow, and quantity. This can create tremendous stress among those around them. Another constant plague is mixed signals: starting one thing and either getting redirected, misdirected, or losing interest altogether. Again, this can be quite frustrating to colleagues and subordinates. If the ENFP is the top dog in the organization, his or her tendency to generate ideas or alternatives constantly—few of which may represent more than thinking out loud—is yet another source of frustration, especially to Judgers.

Their hunger for the excitement of the new and different can lead ENFPs to respond to the brushfires of the moment, to the neglect of ongoing duties and responsibilities. This sometimes misplaced enthusiasm can lead to the wide mood swings already mentioned and may result in any of the three physical maladies common to both ENFPs and their first cousin, the ENTP: headaches, upper back and neck pain, and extreme fatigue. With each day a series of more starts than finishes, the ENFP ultimately becomes unstable, undependable, fickle, and easily discouraged. It is the ENFP of whom it was stated, "The road to hell is paved with good intentions."

When an ENFP successfully settles in on one of the many career choices that may be at his or her disposal, the ENFP's greatest reward will come from those careers that allow free and nonbureaucratic response in some sort of service to humanity. ENFPs excel especially in independent sales, public relations, pediatrics, psychiatry, general family medicine, and almost anything entrepreneurial.

ENTP

Progress Is the Product

When there's an ENTP on the job, one truly does not know what to expect next. It seems like every moment can be up for grabs when this generally high-energy, dynamic, creative, resilient, argumentative type is around. They are the embodiment of "If at first you don't succeed, drop it or try something else." Upbeat, maybe even tiring to different types, ENTPs are the perfect punsters. They would much rather engage in intellectual banter than complete some meaningless task or be quiet by themselves.

For the ENTP the public world is an exciting one (Extraversion). If things aren't exciting, the ENTP will likely want to go out there and make it so, because the external world is full of endless possibilities, random abstractions, and theoretical connections (iNtuition). These perceptions are filtered through objective, impersonal decisions (Thinking), none of which are terribly binding because each day brings new options, open-endedness, and spontaneity (Perception). Hence, while ENTPs can be exciting, they may not be terribly committed to a schedule or project if a better deal or a more exciting challenge comes along en route. It's the nature of the ENTP to be living on the edge of the future, and sometimes the present—always expecting, frequently achieving, and certainly changing each situation. Change for the sake of change will teach everyone involved something, even if it is only the reality that the change was a bad one. The experience of learning even that will have made it all worthwhile. Following a star that ultimately goes nowhere is often better than being bound by a routine or caught up in some form of dullness or doing something that involves no learning at all.

The ENTP female's lot can be a difficult one because she is frequently greatly removed from any stereotypical expectations. She is driven by all the argumentativeness and chutzpah that go with this type. Qualities that will not endear her to her colleagues in the workplace include intellectual arrogance, impatience when things aren't readily understood, arguing for the sake of provoking thought, and talking out of both sides of her mouth in the effort to stimulate conversation. The ENTP commits this "dualspeak" to make others think, but it can be frequently misperceived as flighty at best and downright obnoxious at worst. Whatever, it's certainly not feminine. Actually it's very ENTP and generally great fun. It's just that traditional organizations do not expect females to behave in this way, so ENTP females must compromise their natural skills and abilities for some form of social acceptance—or let the chips fall where they may, alienating the traditionalists. Occasionally such direct behavior can be seen as heroic by those who befriend the ENTP female. When her attributes are appreciated, the ENTP female can provide a significant contribution to the work force as well as an inspirational challenge to most projects to be done.

ENTP males generally have a great deal going for themselves and are appreciated for their enthusiasm and intellectual insights. Their argumentativeness is frequently accepted as part of a male role, and their visionary nature is considered an asset. Perhaps the most negative issue centers around their Perceiving lifestyle—particularly their spontaneity and disdain for routine. For a heavily structured organization, such behaviors can be disjointing, to say the least, and counterproductive when deadlines loom. However, though occasionally frowned upon for such behaviors, the ENTP male still receives much more acceptance in the workplace than his female counterpart.

Interestingly, when either male or female ENTPs come to terms with the organization, they are frequently promoted to the highest levels. Their inspirational vision outweighs any of the problems mentioned above.

The ENTP tends to see the workplace—indeed the entire world—as one large board upon which the daily game of life is played. The game is never over. There are some wins and losses, but mostly it is one exciting challenge after another. The important thing is the challenge, not the outcome. "Did you learn something in the process?" "Is life (the workplace) better off because of the process?" "Has there been some kind of movement, some genuine reevaluation in the process?" "How ready are you to take on tomorrow because of what you've learned today?" These are all semi-rhetorical questions that underlie most of the ENTP's energy for daily work.

As a rule ENTPs can be quite competitive and very freewheeling. As such they are more architects—who draw rough plans so that people and things can be shaped and reshaped daily—than hands-on builders concerned about the details that turn such plans into action. They have a naturally inquisitive personality that, if not recognized, can drive others crazy. They will "Why?" or "Why not?" a situation, even a completed one, to death. As Extraverts they are prone to overkill; combined with their iNtuitive-Thinking-Perception, they sometimes lack good social timing and as a result end up beating dead horses, arguing subjects long ago resolved, or revisiting sore or sensitive subjects at inappropriate times.

While ENTPs would rather be the one to come out on top in any sort of argument or engagement (Who wouldn't? The Introverted-Sensing-Feeler, that's who), the exchange itself may be compensation enough. While losing may be frustrating, the ENTP's respect for the individual who engaged him or her will likely be enhanced.

ENTPs are idea people. Their single greatest contribution to life and work is the creation of ideas. These flow from the ENTP continuously. ENTPs are entrepreneurs who are always sharing or selling their next great idea and attempting to generate some enthusiastic support for it. The more the ENTP extraverts, the more life becomes visions and possibilities. ENTPs can have an uncanny knack for predicting trends in the marketplace or products of the future or other designs for work, play, or home. No sooner does the idea flash through an ENTP's mind than it is instantly added to or enhanced. It may then be dropped should a new idea forge its way forward. To start the day with one or two ideas, engage or be engaged by others, and end the day with five or six ideas, is exhilarating to the ENTP. Though frequently the ideas may be within the expertise of the ENTP, they are not necessarily limited to it. As a result ENTPs really do broad-brush life, probably giving a whole lot more than they take, creating more than implementing, starting more than finishing. But that is their excitement as well as their contribution.

Another ENTP strength is their visionary enthusiasm for most of life. At their best they hear a drumbeat from the future. ENTPs live the science fiction, that which the rest of the world calls farfetched but that eventually catches up with us. The twenty-first century happens now, because ENTP visionaries stretch the commonplace and make it happen. Don't tell an ENTP that we can't fly a rocket to Mars, build a 200-story skyscraper, or communicate over two-way wrist radios. That will be an invitation for the ENTP to prove you wrong. And in the process a new invention or some small step for humankind may result. Never content with the ordinary, always restless with the mundane, ENTPs put meat on the skeletons of society's ideas. Such visionary behavior is not only infectious but readily becomes the core of growth for the next generation. We change, grow, develop, and break through to new frontiers because ENTPs are the ones that force such ideas upon the rest of the world.

Still another strength of the ENTP is their zest for life. Everything is an excuse to engage others. Where ENTPs are concerned, even "reflective listening" can be a competitive sport. Academically alert, ENTPs often have diverse interests. Fed by their idea-generating nature, these ideas spill over into a constant drive for competency and capability in a wide range of interests. It's common for them to carry on many projects at once, not always related to one another. Simultaneously they can have a hobby that's very removed from their vocation. On top of all this they can be engaged in one or more community or social functions. To each of these they will bring high energy, imagination, and creativity that will reflect a great deal of competence. While others can tire of or be tired by the ENTPs' upbeat nature, they will still be inspired by their presence.

Perhaps another strength is their relentless drive for competency in themselves and others. To see life as a daily challenge; to compete, stretch, share, and learn; always to strive to improve oneself and others—these qualities can't help but have a positive impact. It's part of the mystique of the ENTP that they push onward and upward for better and better, never satisfied but always trying to make what's good even better. Such a spirit captivates every entrepreneur, and it's just such a drive for more and more competency that gives birth to zany ideas, brings them to fruition, and moves the world a little farther. Of course not everyone wants to be—or needs to be—improved upon. And colleagues and subordinates can easily tire of the ENTP's restlessness and insatiable appetite for improvement. That can lead to frustration and low morale on the part of the rank and file—ironically the antithesis of what the ENTP was trying to do.

A marked weakness of the ENTP can be their inability to follow through on their exciting ideas. If anyone has ever had an ENTP boss, each day can start with a project, only to be interrupted by another, and still another, leading to frustration and a certain gun-shyness about never knowing what's coming next. At their worst ENTPs are a rage of ideas with little or no follow-through. It is this sort of ENTP that earns the label *underachiever*. They have so much going for them but often deliver so little in terms of measurable results. When ENTPs continue in this pattern, they can even delude themselves into thinking they have implemented or completed a project when they haven't, only to the dismay and disillusionment of those around them.

Another significant downside is the extreme mood swings that can mark their day-to-day existence. ENTPs tend to be extremists at almost everything, and their moods are no exception. Hence, they have higher highs and lower lows than other types, and these swings can occur at a moment's notice. In one breath the ENTP can go from the entrepreneur par excellence to a fickle, depressed, discouraged, self-blaming ne'er-do-well for whom no good word could be spoken. When they hit bottom, they only "yes, but . . ." any encouraging words with lengthy lists of reasons that "prove" their failure and incompetency.

Still another serious flaw among ENTPs is their inability to cope effectively with facts and reality. When details and deadlines pile up, the ENTP can either run away to a new idea or deal with only part of the situation. They then use that part to seduce themselves into thinking that the entire project is completed. The result is at best a half-done job, at worst a total failure, either of which undermines the ENTP's sense of competency and leaves him or her seriously wanting. ENTPs have real trouble tackling only a piece of a problem; they'd rather solve the puzzle in one fell swoop. Failing that, they tend to take flight, neglecting the matter altogether. It's hard for them to see that tending to the little pieces will ultimately solve the whole puzzle.

As with other types the ENTPs' contributions seriously outweigh their liabilities. However, liabilities cannot be denied, or they will become stumbling blocks, tripping them up or leading to ineffectiveness. Through heightened awareness, ENTPs and those with whom they interact will be more readily able to benefit from this type's contributions.

ESTJ

Life's Natural Administrators

More than most other types, the ESTJ is the proverbial jack-of-all-trades. Given to accountability, responsibility, productivity, and results, this type is remarkable at just about anything they do. You can find them in leadership positions in a cross-section of professions, from law and medicine to education and engineering.

Outgoing, gregarious, usually quite direct, and very upbeat to be around (Extraversion), ESTJs see the world in terms of hands-on, practical, realistic situations (Sensing). Those perceptions are translated into objective, nonpersonal, analytical decisions (Thinking) and freely imposed upon anyone within earshot (Judging)—always for someone else's good, of course.

This combination of preferences gives ESTJs a propensity for seeing a situation as it is and moving themselves and others to develop a series of procedures, rituals, or regulations that will not only take care of the situation at hand but will also provide a framework for any future similar situations. It is this special combination of hands-on perception and analytical judgment, focused outward and set in a lifestyle of structure, schedule, and order, that makes ESTJs the administrators of the world. If you want a job done, a regulation established, a system implemented, or an ongoing program evaluated, call on an ESTJ to manage it.

If anything gets them into trouble, it tends to be their EJ attitude toward life, a type given to freely expressed opinions. They can be surprised when others see things differently, and that can lead to some hearty, even abrasive, arguments. From the ESTJ's perspective, it's an open-and-shut case. Having packaged the argument so neatly and precisely, how could anyone possibly disagree? Indeed, from an ESTJ's perspective, most intelligent people would want to get "on board" and take advantage of the ESTJ's homework.

As a general rule ESTJs will rise to the top of almost any organization. When this isn't the case, it's usually because their EJ orientation has alienated others or their argumentative nature has made enemies of someone higher up. If they manage to keep this behavior in check and can show their expertise without accompanying impatience toward those who do not readily see how capable they are, then they are a natural to achieve leadership roles. They often do well academically, which allows them to carry the proper credentials, and they use those credentials in a very authoritative way, demanding respect. If Joe or Jane Smith has earned a Ph.D., and you were to address him or her as Mr. or Ms. Smith, you would be instantly corrected: "That's *Doctor* Smith." (Similarly it's the ESTJ who will identify himself as "Capt. Joseph E. Smith III, USN, Ret.") ESTJs command—and demand—respect from others, and they give it to others when appropriate.

ESTJ women face particular and unique problems. We've said all along that T women swim upstream because life in general, and the workplace in particular, does not look kindly upon objective, hard-thinking females. In this case, as Extraverted-Thinking types, they are not only objective in their decision making, they are also up-front and outgoing about those decisions—often to the intimidation of many.

Complicating matters are the two conflicting roles suggested by the ESTJ's four preferences. On the one hand their Extraverted-Thinking management style is to "take names and kick ass." On the other hand, their Sensing-Judging preferences call upon them to be traditionalists. For women, "tradition" is for them to be caretaking, nurturing defenders of home and hearth. That they instead are top dog within some organizational structure flies in the face of that tradition. The result is an ongoing war raging within some ESTJ women between what they would like to do (be leaders at work) and what they "should" be doing (taking care of the kids at home). Some women compensate at work by dressing and behaving in a way that is ultrafeminine: wearing lots of lace and pink outfits, being soft-spoken, appearing petite, and using a flowing handwriting. However dressed, the female ESTJ's inner conflict can manifest itself in a variety of mixed signals. For example, she may proffer a direct and harsh command with a soft-spoken voice or dole out a compliment in a seemingly cold, offhand way. Such comments may be perfectly acceptable when coming from a male. When done by a female (especially one dressed in frilly pink), they not only raise eyebrows, they also tend to affirm self-doubt, insecurity, and ambivalence within the ESTJ herself.

Should an ESTJ overcome this internal tug-of-war, and should she find acceptance within the workplace, the ESTJ woman will demand the same respect as her male counterpart. If so, there's nothing to say that ESTJ women can't be just as effective at any of the professional areas to which they may gravitate.

Because they are more common than any other type— in the United States there are more Extraverts, Sensors, Thinking males, and Judgers—ESTJ males fit most of the corporate norms, even the statistical ones. They tend to be white, male, appropriate dressers, trustworthy, loyal, reverent, and to possess most of the other Boy Scout traits. To them such norms underscore their belief that "that's the way life should be," an attitude they freely impose on others.

Because ESTJs are a take-charge type with very high control needs and because of their severe sense of accountability, they do not cope well when things do not go as planned. They have no tolerance for disorganization, tardiness, sloppiness, or inappropriate behavior (as defined by the ESTJ). All are invitations for a barrage of criticism. ESTJs have a short fuse when anything suggests they are losing control. The ESTJ can become loud, rigid, domineering, and can induce a great deal of stress within anyone nearby. (As a rule ESTJs are ulcer givers, not ulcer getters.) Not that this is malevolent. Indeed it is intended to further what seems to be a self-ordained mission to keep the world running and to keep people doing what they should be doing.

Because of this, ESTJs can have real trouble listening to subordinates, or anyone else whom they define as unqualified to render an opinion. This includes children and others outside the chain of command. ESTJs understand how the bureaucracy functions and work it to the max.

The ESTJ's chain-of-command mentality may produce behavior that on the surface seems inconsistent with the ESTJ's everyday style. Hard-charging, take-charge, high-ranking ESTJs can appear almost milquetoast at home or in social gatherings. Once the ESTJ decrees that the home is the spouse's turf (or the party is the host's turf), that spouse (or host) is in charge. According to the chain of command, the spouse (host) should give the orders, and the ESTJ will follow quite obediently. Hours later, back at work, it is once again time to turn the tables and take over. What is important to realize is that neither of these seemingly contradictory behaviors is inconsistent with being an ESTJ.

Their innate compulsivity makes it difficult for ESTJs to relax. It's been said that they are capable of turning reading into a competitive sport. In later life this can manifest itself in a variety of stress-related health problems and make retirement difficult and intimidating.

As they progress through life—and up the organizational ladder—ESTJs would do well to mellow themselves by exploring areas contrary to their everyday styles and experiences—for example the soft sciences, such as psychology and sociology, as well as literature, art, and music. All may provide insights and inspiration that can help ESTJs to respect others' points of view and to appreciate that there is more to life than compulsive deadlines.

ESFJ

Everyone's Trusted Friend

Graciousness describes the general lifestyle of the ESFJ, and it also sums up their management style. From separating conflicted workers to overseeing the company Christmas party, the ESFJ brings an appropriateness and graciousness to whatever is demanded. Such a quality is both an asset and a liability. It's an asset because ESFJs motivate and encourage workers to accomplish goals, and the work setting is a very pleasant one, albeit somewhat formal. The liability can result in the ESFJ's allowing himself or herself to be taken advantage of constantly.

ESFJs are socially gregarious (Extravert), which is manifested especially in the precious attention they pay to both organizational and personal details (Sensing). All of this happens in an interpersonal style given to praise and other affirmations (Feeling) against a backdrop of structure, schedule, and order (Judging). It is the ESFJ manager who will remember names and birthdays and do little niceties throughout the workday. When one works for an ESFJ, he or she is usually quite sure of what the ESFJ appreciates and what tasks have been performed well. However, one also knows when a mistake has been made. The ESFJ's parental judgment, even impatience, is apparent even if no words have been spoken.

It is a Santa Claus management style, in which the ESFJ keeps lists, even mental ones, and checks them twice, noting who's been naughty and who's been nice. Score is kept by an ESFJ manager; it's part of the turf. Rewards are forthcoming for good work and critical glances and guilt trips can accompany misplaced work assignments and energies.

Gender issues are a factor among ESFJs, but in very unexpected ways. For one thing it is almost impossible to find a female ESFJ beyond middle management. The ESFJ is very traditional and formal, and in keeping with those traditions upper management is considered "a man's job." These traditions are so strong that they are followed even by ESFJ females themselves, who may likely turn down a promotion, preferring a man to fill that role. In jobs where ESFJ females predominate—teaching, nursing, real estate, and sales—they still frequently refuse the promotion to top positions in favor of males. Such refusal, while frustrating to other non-ESFJ females, plays marvelously into all of the ESFJ's expectations, values, and traditions.

For the male ESFJ it's a very different story. Their traditionalism tells them they should compete and rise to top positions. As a result they may be found across all levels of management, and in higher positions their competitive drive can make them appear to be super-macho among other men. In women's presence, in contrast, they are prone to behave strictly "by the rules," with nary a misspoken word or other inappropriate behavior. All of this is done with ease and facility, which makes them quite acceptable to a broad spectrum of types.

Those who manage to catch the male ESFJ at both acts— one minute acting tough and drinking beer with the boys, the next minute appearing suave and gallant among the ladies—may well conclude that the ESFJ is two-faced, perhaps phony, and not to be trusted. This is a false assumption, and should the ESFJ get wind of it, he will likely feel severely wounded, having considered himself to be of extremely high integrity. It is very important for the ESFJ male to recognize this possibility and to do what is necessary to head off such perceptions. Others must understand that this behavior results from a dichotomy between the Sensing-Judging traditionalism and the Extraverted-Feeling need to affirm everyone according to his or her differences. Although these conflicting forces may seem irreconcilable, to the ESFJ, they're not. In fact to the ESFJ, relating differently to each individual is part of the awesome responsibility of effective leadership.

The ESFJ's strengths are many and varied. They are punctual, neat, responsible, and highly productive, with a great concern for others. In no time they can become the institutional memory and can generally achieve a favorable balance between the people being managed (process) and the tasks to be accomplished (product). These things combined make them friendly motivators for whom to work. They know when to push the work force, when to hold the line and be firm, and when to back off and socialize. A sense of duty, loyalty, and ethical commitment to the organization are embedded deeply in the ESFJ's management style. They live and work that way—and expect others to do the same. Such commitment can at times make them seem like slaves to the organization. The ESFJ would see no problem with that description and would wonder why everyone isn't similarly inclined.

All of these qualities, while certainly admirable, can also set ESFJs up for some serious problems. For example their good nature seems to be constantly tested by others. And when pushed to the limit, ESFJs are more likely to acquiesce than to hold fast. That's doubly problematic for the ESFJ: Not only are they taken advantage of in the workplace but the residual anger may be carried home and directed to friends or family members. In either case it is an issue that ought to have been dealt with at work. Moreover ESFJs' sense of appropriateness can, when pushed to the limit, make them appear rigid and closed to new ideas.

When backed into such a corner it is the ESFJ more than other types who is prone to induce guilt and shame as a way of making colleagues or subordinates respond. They can turn into the stereotypical Jewish mother—"After all I've done for you . . ."—which is neither becoming nor appropriate, especially at work.

Perhaps even more serious is the ESFJ's proclivity to avoid conflict. They would rather deny something's wrong than confront it. When a disagreement occurs, it is particularly ESFJ to sweep it under the rug. Failing this, an ESFJ will be inclined to buy everyone a cup of coffee (or chicken soup or beer), sit around a table, and say, "There, there. We're all friends. Everything's okay. What's the big deal?" A simple raising of the voice in a hearty argument or simple disagreements can be interpreted by an ESFJ as extreme hostility and ultimately destructive to relationships and productivity. Such a reaction generally renders the ESFJ somewhere between traumatic ineptitude and total frozen incompetency. What may seem to be a harmless yet necessary process—simple day-to-day discussions that move the organization toward its goals—can result in the ESFJ losing control and can leave them feeling very incapable. It may be nothing short of a terrifying experience.

ESFJs need to realize that conflict and disagreement are a part of everyday activity. They must understand that they will be respected far more for sticking to their guns than by caving in to other points of view in the name of harmony. They need to remind themselves constantly that conflict and disharmony can ultimately lead a group to increased creativity and productivity. Most of all, ESFJs must continually remind themselves in such situations that the disharmony is generally not a reflection on them and that seeing it through to a solution is better for all involved.

Given such responsibility and nurturing tendencies, the ESFJ can become stressed when people do not live up to what the ESFJ defines as appropriate and responsible. For someone in authority to tell the ESFJ not to worry about such things only adds to the ESFJ's tension; "not worrying" becomes another thing to worry about. Instead ESFJs need to talk things through with others. They especially need support, encouragement, and social connections during stressful situations, even though their own tendency would be to deny such support or to feel unworthy of it. Hard work, even busywork, is better than sitting around alone imagining the worst. Diverting the stress energy into some meaningful activity with measurable results and positive social reinforcement is probably as effective as any stress-reducing technique for this type.

Careers in which ESFJs excel include the social services—public health and social welfare agencies, for example—sales (especially real estate), school administration, and clergy. All of these areas allow ESFJs to maximize their natural talents to be gregarious, interpersonally skilled, organized, and focused upon others' needs. In addition, because ESFJs, more than other types, often find themselves in careers that result from emulating childhood role models, they can and do work well in many other fields for which they would not normally seem appropriate, including accounting, law, and engineering.

ENFJ

Smooth-Talking Persuaders

If you need to sell the impossible to a reluctant buyer and make the buyer like it, then you'll do no better than to call upon an ENFJ. These smooth-talking persuaders are life's salespeople, and once an ENFJ is convinced that you need the product in question, you will become putty in the ENFJ's hands. He or she will combine the perfect combination of words and rapport to clinch the deal.

Each of the ENFJ's preferences compound to make them a natural convincer. Their energy comes from the outwardly directed, socially oriented, gregarious external world (Extraversion). They prefer to perceive the world as having endless possibilities and meanings (iNtuition), which they use to make subjective, interpersonally based decisions (Feeling). They prefer to live their daily lives in a structured, scheduled, and orderly fashion (Judging).

When the ENFJ scans a situation, he or she is often aware of the many interpersonal dynamics that may be taking place. From the start, their iNtuitive preference interprets each party's actions and reactions—who seems stressed, who may need to be motivated, who should be reprimanded, who needs a listening ear—with their Judging preference providing direction or suggestions as appropriate, at least in the ENFJ's mind. Frequently their advice is apt, which engenders both gratitude and dependence on the ENFJ. When an individual or group doesn't pick up on the ENFJ's advice, the ENFJ can, in a moment, become bruised and angry at such ingratitude.

ENFJ females tend to fit in well at work. They possess a good sense of propriety, fulfilling a great deal of socially expected *shoulds* and *oughts*, not necessarily because they want to but because, as Extraverted-Feelers, they have a high need to please others. Generally they present a pleasant and acceptable image, acting out their natural caring and concern for others. Often they will be perceived as popular female role models, something they enjoy and espouse. If the ENFJ female has a failing, it may be when her idealism leads her to take a rigid stand on some issue, alienating others in the process. While her male counterparts are equally likely to do this, such behavior seems out of character for women at work.

ENFJ men, on the other hand, face more serious problems at work. They are confronted with the struggles of all Feeling-type males in the workplace: being perceived as tenderhearted, nurturing, and even wimpy. Consequently ENFJ males are torn between imitating a more traditional male role model (an imitation they can do very well) or giving in to their more natural preferences and risking being labeled as effeminate. If they opt for the macho role, their behavior may be accompanied by guilt and ambiguity about their identity. If they choose the more natural route, their masculinity may be called into question, leading to a variety of sexually seductive games intended to prove their manhood. In either case it's a serious struggle for the ENFJ male. One way they resolve the struggle is to be drawn toward careers involving psychology, theology, and other "people-oriented" issues. These professions are largely male-dominated, with a female aura to them: nurturing, caring, self-extension, martyrdom, sacrifice—all noble, but largely traditionally feminine attributes.

The overall work style of the ENFJ is upbeat, affirming, and usually marked with an above-average social awareness. Their iNtuition tends to keep them enthusiastic, even when the task may be somewhat dull or routine. ENFJs can seem like cheerleaders in such situations, calling forth others' loyalty, perseverance, humor, or whatever else may be needed when the chips are down. This is done by maintaining a positive outlook and generously affirming others. In fact, if they are not careful, ENFJs can be dubbed superficial by others, who see the affirmations as nothing but cheap talk. When this happens, ENFJs are cut to the quick, because they felt they were doing their best for the good of the cause, only to be shot down. Work should be a team effort, says the ENFJ, no matter what it is. And people need to be happy with one another, caring well beyond their individual job descriptions. It's "Go, team, go" from nine to five, followed by a beer or two together and anything else that will affirm the group and its capabilities. ENFJs have a listening ear for others' troubles and may even be offended if one isn't willing to bare all. That's what friends are for.

While all Feeling types prefer a happy, harmonious work environment, the ENFJ has an unusually strong need to be the one who leads the work force to this goal. However, for all their good intentions, they can run afoul of others, particularly other Extraverted-Judgers, who may also be vying to take charge.

As a Judging type the ENFJ usually has enough natural need for closure that deadlines get met and production requirements get fulfilled, though some immediate interpersonal need or human need may momentarily sidetrack them. This makes ENFJs very promotable within the organizational hierarchy. What usually motivates the ENFJ to climb the ladder, however, is not mere good behavior so much as having a vision that organizations exist to serve people. Inevitably, as they accept promotions, they find themselves at odds with corporate realities: profits, productions, cutbacks, and the like. The more ENFJs rise to the loftier positions within the organization, the more they may be setting themselves up for a struggle between their personal demands and organizational demands. At the higher levels such issues won't go away by themselves, nor can they be swept under the rug, as the ENFJ would prefer to do. For everyone involved, it will be much more productive if an ENFJ could be more in touch with his or her real drives and motivations and could consider whether they are realistic in terms of the organization's mission. This could save personal—and even organizational—heartburn.

One of the strengths of ENFJs is their capacity to inspire others. ENFJs have been called life's teachers. To the degree that teaching, leading, and working with others to accomplish something involves understanding others' needs, finding the exact words to inspire, and the appropriate affirmations along the way, ENFJs are naturals: Their Extraversion focuses the attention on others; their iNtuition can prove inspirational and encouraging, especially when things may be going badly; their Feeling serves as a constant barometer, sensitive to the people and the situation; and their Judging keeps the entire process task-oriented so that upon completion, everyone will have a sense of accomplishment. Generally people can face difficult moments with an ENFJ as a support and end up not only reaching a goal handily but coming to enjoy the process of getting there.

Another strength of ENFJs is their interpersonal skills. At their best they can keep any number of people, issues, and events moving toward happy conclusions. ENFJs are good psychologists, with or without training, and generally listen well to others' problems. They can also conciliate stressful situations that may be blocking productivity. (They are usually better at this conciliation when they are not personally involved.) All of this serves to make ENFJs natural sounding boards for just about everyone in the organization, a position that most ENFJs readily enjoy.

Still another strength of ENFJs is their ability to present organizational values for both the work force and the public in such a way that all parties benefit. ENFJs are political animals whose mission it is to define life's values, and provide leadership in shaping those values. More often than not, those values will be centered around interpersonal issues: making the world a safer place to live, making the workplace more congenial, having the organization do well by doing good. Hence, when an ENFJ is present, no matter what the product or mission, the people involved will be important and the human dynamic will be made a central part of the process. ENFJs often become the organizational conscience.

One of the drawbacks of ENFJs is the facility with which they can overpersonalize negative reactions to their ideas and ideals. "If people are not motivated by me or not open with me, then somehow I have failed," the ENFJ believes. The ENFJ can then become filled with a sense of inadequacy and can be almost incapable of proceeding. An individual who shares a personal problem or experience with a group could lead an ENFJ to wonder, "Why didn't she share it with just me? Doesn't she like me?" In the ENFJ's mind, because the individual in question had previously shared other personal issues, her failure to do it this time reflects the ENFJ's personal failure. This can lead the ENFJ to distrust her, perhaps even projecting that distrust onto others.

Another ENFJ weakness is the almost demonic character they can assume when their values are questioned—or worse, assailed. Should one question or challenge the validity of an ENFJ's motivations, the ENFJ will likely see that as a questioning of their integrity and trustworthiness. And it's downhill from there. It's almost as if the values had been formed by some force greater than the ENFJ, and to go against them is to go against the universe, in the ENFJ's mind. For example, should a group of co-workers reject the ENFJ's promotion of teamwork as a necessary part of the workplace—"We don't have to like each other to get the job done," might be their rationale—the ENFJ would probably feel personally attacked and may redouble his or her efforts. These people can become unbelievably rigid, admonishing others, "You are not only going against me on this. You're undermining the moral fiber of the whole organization." It is this overreaction that can lead others to consider the ENFJ fanatic, extremist, or simply overemotional.

A third ENFJ weakness can be a sense of guilt, inadequacy, or failure that can plague them for no apparent reason. ENFJs can be loved and revered by colleagues and staff and yet feel undeserving of such accolades or guilty over unreached goals. When this behavior gets in the way, ENFJs distort issues badly and can move through mood swings that range from "People are no damn good, and no one can be trusted" to "I've got to try harder and harder to get them to love me and my cause."

When such weaknesses can be kept in check, ENFJs can be infectious and inspirational at any level and in almost any job. To the degree that there is a need for teaching, interpersonal concern, and the bringing in of moral values is the degree to which ENFJs will rise to the occasion—and to various levels of leadership and responsibility within the organization.

ENTJ

Life's Natural Leaders

The ENTJ has been called life's natural leader, and that's not by accident. The special combination of preferences gives this type the right mixture of basic leadership qualities: enthusiasm, vision, objectivity, and accountability. So natural are these qualities that it is almost difficult for an ENTJ *not* to step in and take charge. And they do it with such finesse that others tend to appreciate it and begin to depend upon them in any variety of situations. More often than not, the ENTJ is pleased to respond with facility and competence.

Their outer-directed, people-oriented energy (Extraversion) gives them a basic social alertness. They prefer to translate that alertness into possibilities, meanings, and connections (iNtuition) as they deal with their perceptions of events. Those perceptions are then dealt with objectively (Thinking), helping to create a vision, a strategy, or a complex system that will move the organization toward its goal. Their need for closure, structure, and accountability (Judging) makes sure that these visions, strategies, and systems are not left on the drawing board or lost to some abstract inspiration. With ENTJs, they are more likely to become finished products. As a result, it's an onward-and-upward, over-and-over-again kind of existence for all within the ENTJ's sphere of influence.

While all of the aforementioned qualities are indeed marks of a good leader, and while they are universally appreciated and respected, they are most commonly attributed to males. Thus the ENTJ female has a particularly rough course in life, if she has any savvy and gumption. Most of the words used to describe leadership can, with no effort, be interpreted as pushy and overbearing when referring to females. Consider: *take charge, commanding, objective, confrontive, gregarious.* These are just a few of the descriptors that men are lauded for, but for which women can be scorned. The combination of Extraversion, iNtuition, Thinking, and Judging offers all the same behaviors in females as it does in males—strategies, visions, big-picture thinking, and impatience with those who see things differently. But an ENTJ woman is in a special bind. If she gives in to her enthusiasms of the moment, she can become downright intimidating to those present. On the other hand, if she denies these impulses to take charge, she can become impatient and irritable in relegating herself as a quiet, supportive bystander. ENTJ women can overcome this seemingly lose/lose proposition by staying objective in a difficult situation and by recognizing that though things may seem personal, that is probably not the case. They can also thrive by balancing their natural femininity with their natural leadership skills, recognizing that it's okay to exhibit both characteristics in the workplace and that these are in fact synergistic; and by recognizing that many of the problems they encounter are common to all ENTJs, regardless of gender. While these may not be panaceas for all ENTJ problems, they are good starting points.

As Extraverted-Judgers, ENTJs are robust, direct, and hearty strategists. Quickly and keenly ENTJs can see possibilities in almost everything and can act upon those possibilities instantly. They share their directions and opinions quite freely and easily, assuming that anyone who disagrees does so fully ready to engage in meaningful, albeit somewhat confrontive and direct, dialogue. For ENTJs that's how growth happens and mountains are moved. Because the ENTJ is something of a political animal, the communication process is one in which differing points of view are placed squarely on the table and opposing forces go head to head until a resolution is reached. This is a very exciting process to ENTJs. They see daily life as a kind of chessboard, upon which people, things, and entities are moved, removed, altered, and engaged—constantly for the organizational good.

Such objective, removed behavior allows ENTJs to become highly involved in many things and at the same time never really become personally invested in any of them. They can argue—they call it "discuss"—any subject with zeal and not be personally hurt by what's said, annoyed even that someone else may have become bruised in the process. ENTJs are often accused of sounding angry, a reflection of the enthusiasm and directness with which they freely express their opinions, all in the spirit of a healthy exchange. But the ENTJ may be neither angry nor uncaring and may find such an accusation surprising and infuriating. Similarly they can become deeply involved in another's personal trauma yet let it have almost no impact on themselves, a trait not always appreciated by others. An ENTJ might listen to another's tale of woe with genuine empathy, then moments later say something totally unrelated and seemingly uncaring; it's not that the ENTJ doesn't care, it's just that having gotten the problem out and "solved," it is time to move on.

The strengths of the ENTJ include their penchant for handling complexities. While they may go overboard and make even simple things complicated, their uncanny ability to arrange people and things in configurations that motivate and inspire is a rare and unique trait. ENTJs understand that success is measured in terms of what is accomplished, not in terms of how much one is liked by others. As a result they readily accept the hard reality that they may make enemies in making decisions for the good of the organization; like all TJs they would rather be right than liked.

Another strength of ENTJs is their ability to balance a vision of the future with an ability to take risks. Because they are structure oriented, they make better intrapreneurs (working innovatively within an organization) than entrepreneurs (working on one's own). In any case their risk taking is buffered by their need to produce bottom-line results. Unlike their ENTP cousins, who are prone to take more extreme risks—with bigger wins and bigger losses— ENTJs' risks, and rewards, are more moderate. This makes for an acceptable level of instability for the conservative corporate culture of most larger companies.

For the ENTJ all of life is learning, so one is forever a student. Any event that will increase one's mental capabilities—even something as mundane as a freewheeling office discussion—should never be taken lightly and must include intense involvement. Even when the event is over, the ENTJ will likely revisit it, restating what was learned, conceptualizing it, integrating it into the system—in short, beating it to death, at least in others' minds.

ENTJs pride themselves on their independence, and it is a legacy they would give to their subordinates. They want staff to be independent and freethinking and to disdain the "yes man" mentality. It is better to have challenged and lost than never to have challenged at all. The problem is that not everyone wants to be independent and freethinking; some simply want to be told what to do. This frustrates ENTJs to no end. For those who meet the challenge, ENTJs can become quite impatient and intimidating. This dynamic carries on day in and day out, even to those who meet the challenge. Those working with or for an ENTJ inevitably tire of this stress and wonder if there's anything they can do right in the ENTJ's eyes.

ENTJs' biggest drawbacks are their arrogance, their impatience, and their insensitivity. Their objectivity and love for the abstract provides them with a healthy amount of intellectual competence; they usually do well in academic pursuits. But they tend to look down upon those who don't learn or make connections as readily as they do. Because they are Extraverted-Judgers, they are not shy about informing others of their opinions of them. Such arrogance is demeaning to underlings and can cut into morale and productivity.

Similarly, because they have quick minds and readily see what needs to be done to move an organization or system toward progress, they can become abrasive when others aren't equally perceptive. They often have a short fuse for those who want to delay action in favor of more careful review of a proposed plan. Their special combination of preferences often provides them with a good working plan of action. They are often right, and they know it. They view the process of getting others on board as a waste of precious time.

Another waste of time, in the ENTJ's mind, is having to beat around the bush in communicating with others. Their motto: Say what needs to be said, and let the chips fall where they may. Clearly such directness, combined with their arrogance and impatience, can at best bruise egos, at worst cause insurrection. Moreover, having placed themselves as the vocal arbiters of just about everything, they leave little room for their own shortcomings. When they do make mistakes, they tend to admit them with the same directness and arrogance with which they criticize others. Still, the rest of the organization takes great joy in seeing that this paragon of competence is only human.

In short, ENTJs are natural architects, and this in fact is one of the careers in which they abound. But they are not limited to designing buildings. They are equally capable in careers that allow them to design institutions, programs, even people's lives. They make excellent teachers, CEOs, and strategists, whether in the military or in government. Their inquisitiveness makes them natural scientists, lawyers, and journalists.

ABOUT OTTO KROEGER ASSOCIATES

Otto Kroeger Associates is a psychological and management consulting firm located in Fairfax, Virginia. We provide consultation and training in organizational development, conflict resolution, goal-setting, and communication to a wide range of organizations, using the Myers-Briggs Type Indicator™ as a basis for understanding differences. It is one of only three organizations certified to provide qualifying training for professionals in administering and interpreting the MBTI. In addition, we have developed a variety of Typewatching™-related materials, including videotapes, audiotapes, and a series of sixteen T-shirts.

WORKSHOPS

• Typewatching Qualifying Workshop: Upon successful completion, participants will be recommended to Consulting Psychologists Press to be "Qualified" to purchase the MBTI.

• Advanced Workshops: Intensive courses for professionals already qualified to use the MBTI.

• Specialized Workshops: Workshops designed to take trainers beyond the basics to specific uses within organizations.

ALSO FROM OTTO KROEGER ASSOCIATES

• *Type Talk At Work: How the 16 Personality Types Determine Your Success on the Job*, by Otto Kroeger with Janet M. Thuesen—the complete 400-page book from which these 16 profiles were excerpted.

• *Type Talk: The 16 Personality Types that Determine How We Live, Love, and Work,* by Otto Kroeger and Janet M. Thuesen —the ultimate guide on how to use Typewatching™ in all parts of your life.

• *Typewatching . . . A Byte at a Time* — an exciting MBTI™ learning tool for IBM–compatible computers. Learn about the preferences, types, and how they interact at work, home, and at play.

• All the best books on Jungian theory and the MBTI™.

• Typewatching™ tape series — 16 cassettes, one on each type.

• 16 different Typewatching™ T-Shirts ... and More!

FOR MORE INFORMATION, WRITE OR CALL
Otto Kroeger Associates • 3605 Chain Bridge Rd.
Fairfax, VA 22030 • 703-591-MBTI

WE TRAIN THE TRAINERS

to Kroeger Associates offers a number of diverse workshops and a consulting
vices in the area of organizational development. For information, call our
aining Coordinator at 703-591-MBTI.

Our consultants come from diverse backgrounds, including organizational
velopment, counseling, university faculties, psychology, the military, and pri-
e industry. Here is what some have said about what they liked about their
ining at Otto Kroeger Associates:

TJ: "The hands–on exercises and practical applications."

FJ: "Learning more about myself than I could have anticipated."

TP: "The wealth of practical applications offered by the instructors."

FP: "Nice warm training atmosphere. Five days and never a dull moment. I loved it all."

TP: "Trainers' styles and abilities to teach all types."

FP: "Nice people, highly energetic and informed trainers who respected the group. They really practiced what they preached."

TJ: "The teachers, the orderly flow of the training, the variety of learning activities, and the food."

FJ: "The friendly atmosphere—the sheer fun approach to learning in a relaxed style; the weird hats."

FJ: "The nonstop immersion in MBTI. It is a part of your lives, and you invited us in as if introducing us to a close friend."

TJ: "It answered all my questions and then some. I'll be back."

FP: "The chance to be myself among many quite different."

TP: "The interaction between types. It was the first time I had seen SJs in the minority."

FP: "Stories, anecdotes, and wonderful personal insights."

TP: "The theory."

FJ: "Expertise of the trainers—the best I've ever seen—and the commitment of the entire staff."

TJ: "Brilliant leadership and ethical sensitivity by the trainers. A first–rate experience."